EYEWITNESS
HUMAN BODY

Fertilization of a human egg

Bone micro-structure

Red blood cells

Fingerprint

Bone saw

Spinal cord

Human skeleton

ompound microscope

EYEWITNESS
HUMAN
BODY

Written by
Richard Walker

Nerve cell

Respiratory system

DK

Chromosome

19th-century clamping forceps

LONDON, NEW YORK, MUNICH,
MELBOURNE, AND DELHI

Editor Lisa Stock
Project editor Jane Yorke
Art editor David Ball
Senior editor Rob Houston
Senior art editor Alison Gardner
Managing editor Camilla Hallinan
Managing art editor Owen Peyton Jones
Art director Martin Wilson
Category publisher Andrew Macintyre
Picture researcher Louise Thomas
Production editor Hitesh Patel
Senior production controller Pip Tinsley
Jacket designer Andy Smith
Jacket editor Adam Powley

RELAUNCH EDITION (DK UK)
Editor Ashwin Khurana
Managing editor Gareth Jones
Managing art editor Philip Letsu
Publisher Andrew Macintyre
Producer, pre-production Nikoleta Parasaki
Senior producer Charlotte Cade
Jacket editor Maud Whatley
Jacket designer Laura Brim
Jacket design development manager Sophia MTT
Publishing director Jonathan Metcalf
Associate publishing director Liz Wheeler
Art director Phil Ormerod

RELAUNCH EDITION (DK INDIA)
Senior editor Neha Gupta
Senior art editor Ranjita Bhattacharji
Senior DTP designer Harish Aggarwal
DTP designer Pawan Kumar
Managing editor Alka Thakur Hazarika
Managing art editor Romi Chakraborty
CTS manager Balwant Singh
Jacket editorial manager Saloni Singh
Jacket designers Suhita Dharamjit, Amit Varma

First published in Great Britain in 2009.
This relaunch edition published in 2014
by Dorling Kindersley Limited, 80 Strand, London WC2R 0RL

Copyright © 2009 © 2014 Dorling Kindersley Limited
A Penguin Company

2 4 6 8 10 9 7 5 3 1
270658 – 11/14

Some of the material in this book previously appeared in
Eyewitness Human Body, published in 1993, 2004.

A CIP catalogue record for this book is available from the British Library.

ISBN 978-0-2410-1361-8

Colour reproduction by Alta Image Ltd, London, UK
Printed and bound by South China Printing Co Ltd, China

Discover more at
www.dk.com

Adult teeth

Heart

Cross-section of the skin

Oxygen-rich blood   Oxygen-poor blood   Settled blood

Brain from below

Contents

Inside the eye

The human body   6

Myth, magic, and medicine   8

Study and dissection   10

The microscopic body   12

Looking inside the body   14

The body's framework   16

Inside bones   18

The body's joints   20

Muscle power   22

The moving body   24

The nervous system   26

The brain   28

Inside the brain   30

Skin and touch   32

Eyes and seeing   34

Ears and hearing   36

Smell and taste   38

Hormones   40

The heart   42

In circulation   44

The blood   46

Breathing to live   48

Inside the lungs   50

Eating   52

Digestion   54

Waste disposal   56

Male and female   58

A new life   60

Growth and development   62

Future bodies   64

Timeline   66

Find out more   68

Glossary   70

Index   72

The human body

We may look different from the outside, but our bodies are all constructed in the same way. The study of anatomy, which explores body structure, shows that internally we are virtually identical – apart from differences between males and females. The study of physiology, which deals with how the body works, reveals how body systems combine to keep our cells, and us, alive.

Human origins
Human beings are all related. We belong to the species *Homo sapiens*, and are descendants of the first modern humans, who lived in Africa 160,000 years ago and migrated across the globe.

Understanding anatomy
The modern study of anatomy dates back to the Renaissance period, in the 15th and 16th centuries. For the first time, it became legal to dissect, or cut open, a dead body in order to examine its parts in minute detail and make accurate drawings.

Muscular system

Skeletal system

The body as a building
In 1708, physiologists likened the body to a busy household – bringing in supplies (eating food), distributing essentials (the blood system), creating warmth (body chemical processes), and organizing everyone (the brain).

Working together
Our internal organs and systems work together to keep us alive. Bones, muscles, and cartilage provide support and movement. Nerves carry control signals. The heart and blood vessels deliver food everywhere, along with oxygen taken in through the lungs. The result of this cooperation is a balanced internal environment, with a constant temperature of 37°C (98.6°F). This enables cells to work at their best.

Eye is a light-detecting sense organ

Vein carries the blood towards the heart

Artery carries the blood away from the heart

Nerve carries electrical signals to and from the brain

Bone supports the upper arm

Body make-up

It takes around 100 trillion cells to build a human body. There are 200 different types of these microscopic living units, each of which is highly complex. Similar cells join together to make a tissue, two or more tissues form an organ, and linked organs create a system. The body has 12 systems.

Cartilage supports the nose

Teeth cut up food during eating

Neck muscle moves the head

Lung gets oxygen into the body

Heart pumps the blood

Tendon attaches a muscle to bone

Liver cleans the blood

Digestive system

Small intestine

1 System
Along with the digestive system, the other 11 are the skin, skeletal, muscular, nervous, hormonal, circulatory, lymphatic, immune, respiratory, urinary, and reproductive systems. The role of the digestive system is to break down food so it can be used by body cells.

2 Organ
The small intestine is a long digestive tube. It completes the breakdown of food into simple substances, which are absorbed into the blood. Muscle tissue in the wall of the small intestine pushes food along it.

3 Tissue
The lining of the small intestine has millions of microscopic finger-like projections called villi. This epithelial tissue provides a vast surface for absorbing food.

4 Cells
The epithelial cells covering a villus are tightly clumped together, which stops food and digestive juices leaking through to the tissues that support these cells.

5 Chromosome
Every cell has a control centre, called its nucleus, which contains 46 chromosomes. These long threads (coiled up in an X-shape, above) contain coded instructions, called genes, which are needed for building our cells, tissues, organs, and systems.

6 DNA
Each chromosome consists of deoxyribonucleic acid (DNA), a molecule. DNA's twisted strands are linked by chemicals called bases (blue, green, red, yellow). Their sequence provides a gene's coded instructions for building or controlling the body.

Myth, magic, and medicine

Early humans made sculptures and cave paintings of human figures. As civilizations grew, people began to study the world around them and their own bodies more closely, but care for the sick and injured was tied up with myths, superstition, and a belief that gods or demons sent illnesses. The "father of medicine", Greek physician Hippocrates (c. 460–377 BCE) taught that diseases could be identified and treated. In the Roman world, Galen (129–c. 216 CE) set out ideas about anatomy and physiology that would last for centuries. As Rome's power declined, medical knowledge spread east to Persia, developed by physicians such as Avicenna (980–1037 CE).

Prehistoric art
The Aboriginal rock art of Australia has featured X-ray figures showing the internal anatomy of humans and animals for 4,000 years.

Holes in the head

This 4,000-year-old skull from Jericho, in Israel, shows the results of trepanning, or drilling holes in the skull – probably to expose the brain and release evil spirits. Modern surgery uses a similar technique, called craniotomy, to release pressure in the brain caused by bleeding.

Surgical sacrifice
In the 14th and 15th centuries, the Aztecs who dominated Mexico believed the god Huitzilopochtli would make the sun rise and bring them success in battle, if offered daily blood, limbs, and hearts torn from living human sacrifices. From these grisly rituals, the Aztecs learned about the inner organs of the body.

Egyptian embalming
Some 5,000 years ago, the Egyptians believed that a dead body remained home to its owner's soul in the afterlife, but only if preserved as a life-like mummy. Natron, a type of salt, was used to dry out the body to embalm it and stop it rotting.

Internal organs, removed from an opening in the side, were preserved separately in special jars

Brain, regarded as useless, was hooked out through the nostrils and discarded

Heart, seen as the centre of being, was left inside the chest

Chinese channels

Written over 2,300 years ago, *The Yellow Emperor's Classic of Internal Medicine* explains acupuncture treatments, which focus on the flow of chi, or vital energy, along 12 body channels, or meridians. Needles are inserted into the skin along these meridians to rebalance the body forces known as Yin (cool and female) and Yang (hot and male).

Claudius Galen

Born in ancient Greece, Claudius Galen became a towering figure in the study of anatomy, physiology, and medicine in Rome. There, he treated gladiators as a young physician, describing their wounds as "windows into the body". Human dissection was banned, so he studied the anatomy of animals instead. His flawed ideas were accepted without question for 1,500 years.

Galen remained a great influence in Europe and the Islamic world for many centuries

edieval treatments

od-letting, using a knife or a blood-
king worm called a leech, was a
ditional, if brutal, remedy for all
nner of ills in medieval times. Few
sicians tried to see if the treatment
s of any benefit to the patient

Embalming process dried out the muscles, which shrank and exposed the bones

Avicenna, the Persian anatomist, built on the teachings of the Romans and Greeks

Hippocrates believed that physicians should act in their patients' best interests

Saving knowledge

This illustration comes from the 1610 translation of the *Canon Of Medicine*, written by the Persian physician Avicenna in c. 1025. He built on the knowledge of Galen and Hippocrates, whose medical works survived the fall of Rome only because they were taken to Persia, translated, and spread through the Islamic world. Their ideas were reintroduced to Europe after Islam spread to Spain in 711 CE.

Skin became dark and leathery through embalming and age

Toenails, being made of dead cells, remained intact

Study and dissection

Respect for death

For many in the Middle Ages, life was less important than death and ascent into heaven. The body housed the soul, and must not be dissected. This anatomist risked being punished.

A rebirth of the arts, architecture, and science spread across Europe between the 14th and 17th centuries. With the dawn of this Renaissance, the ban on human dissection, the precise cutting open of a body to study its internal structure was relaxed. In Italy, Andreas Vesalius (1514–64) performed careful, accurate dissections and drew his own conclusions, based on his observations, rather than blindly repeating the centuries-old accepted views. By questioning and correcting Galen's teachings, he revolutionized the science of anatomy and initiated a new era in medicine.

Anatomical theatre

Mondino dei Liuzzi (c. 1270–1326), a professor at Bologna, Italy introduced the public dissection of human corpses and is known as the Restorer of Anatomy. By the late 16th century, anatomical theatres were built at numerous universities. This 1610 engraving shows the anatomical theatre at Leiden, in the Netherlands. Spectators in the gallery looked down as the anatomy professor or his assistant carried out a dissection.

Strong, thick metal frame

End screw to remove blade

Break with tradition

Padua was at the forefront of Italian anatomy and medicine when Andreas Vesalius arrived in 1536. His exceptional skills were soon evident, and he soon became professor of anatomy. After translating early medical texts, Vesalius became dissatisfied with the teachings from ancient times. He preferred to believe what he saw in front of him, and set about writing his own book.

First scientific anatomy book

After four years of dissection Vesalius *On the Structure of the Human Body* was published in 1543. The detail text and lifelike-death illustrations caused sensation and outrage.

Subjects for study

Hanged criminals were a steady source of specimens for dissection. In *The Anatomy Lesson of Dr Nicholaes Tulp* (1632), by the Dutch artist Rembrandt, the dissection subject was robber Aris Kindt. Anatomy lessons were training for physicians and surgeons, and were open to any interested members of the public.

Women and anatomy

Until the 19th century, women took on only very minor medical roles, except as midwifes. These Swedish women learning anatomy, in a photograph from about 1880, are probably training for midwifery.

Double-ended small probe

Fine end

Bulbous end

Hooked point

Hooked needle

Wooden handle

Skull removed to expose brain

Blade can be sharpened for use

Scalpel

Needle-like tips

Fine forceps (tweezers)

Ridged, splayed tips for gripping

Clamping forceps

Handles have a scissor design

Muscle layer peeled back

Tools of the trade

These 19th-century surgical instruments each have their own role, from cutting through bones to probing tiny nerves and blood vessels. Today's surgeons use a similar but broader range of instruments, making use of modern technology, such as power saws and laser scalpels.

Wax model

Crafted from wax, this anatomical model shows the dissected head and neck, including muscles, nerves, blood vessels, and the brain. In the 18th and 19th centuries, accurately coloured, three-dimensional models like this one were excellent teaching aids for trainee doctors.

Instruments illustrated in the second edition of Vesalius's book, 1555

ated saw blade

Large bone saw

Tensioning screw to tighten blade

Wooden handle shaped to fit palm of hand

The microscopic body

At the beginning of the 1600s, scientific instrument makers in the Netherlands invented a magnifying device called the microscope. For the first time, scientists used high-quality glass lenses to view objects, illuminated by light, which previously had been far too small to see with the naked eye. Pioneering microscopists showed that living things are made up of much smaller units, which Robert Hook (1635–1703) likened to the cells, or rooms, of monks in a monastery. The term "cells" has been used ever since.

Pioneer histologist

Italy's Marcello Malpighi (1628–94) was the founder of microscopic anatomy and a pioneer of histology, the study of tissues. He was the first to identify capillaries, the tiny blood vessels that connect arteries to veins.

Lens held between two plates

Pin to hold the specimen in place

Screw to bring the specimen into focus

Handle to hold the lens close to the eye

Wide-ranging observer

Antoni van Leeuwenhoek (1632–1723) was a Dutch cloth merchant and self-taught scientist. With his homemade microscopes Leeuwenhoek was the first to observe, among many other things, blood cells and sperm. In 1683 he also spotted, in scrapings from his own teeth, the first bacteria seen by the human eye.

Home-made lenses

In van Leeuwenhoek's day, most microscopes had two lenses, as shown on the right. His version, shown life-size above, had one tiny lens, yet it enabled him to observe cells, tissues, and tiny organisms magnified up to 275 times. He made about 400 microscopes, and helped to establish microscopy as a branch of science.

a b c d e f g h

Microscopic drawings

Today, photography can capture what is viewed under the microscope. Early microscopists used drawings and writing to record what they had seen. This drawing by van Leeuwenhoek records his observation, for the first time, of sperm cells.

Eyepiece lens magnifies the image produced by the objective lens

Lens tube

Powerful objective lens collects light from the specimen to create an image

Stage holds the specimen

Specimen illuminated with light from below

Lens focuses light rays from the mirror

Screw adjusts the stage height for focusing

Mirror reflects light from lamp window

Tripod base

Compound microscope

Van Leeuwenhoek's "simple" microscopes had one lens. Most light microscopes, which use light illuminating the specimen, are compound, using or more lenses. This 19th-century model the basic features found on a modern compound microscope. The specimen is sliced thinly end for light to be shone through it and up through the lenses to the

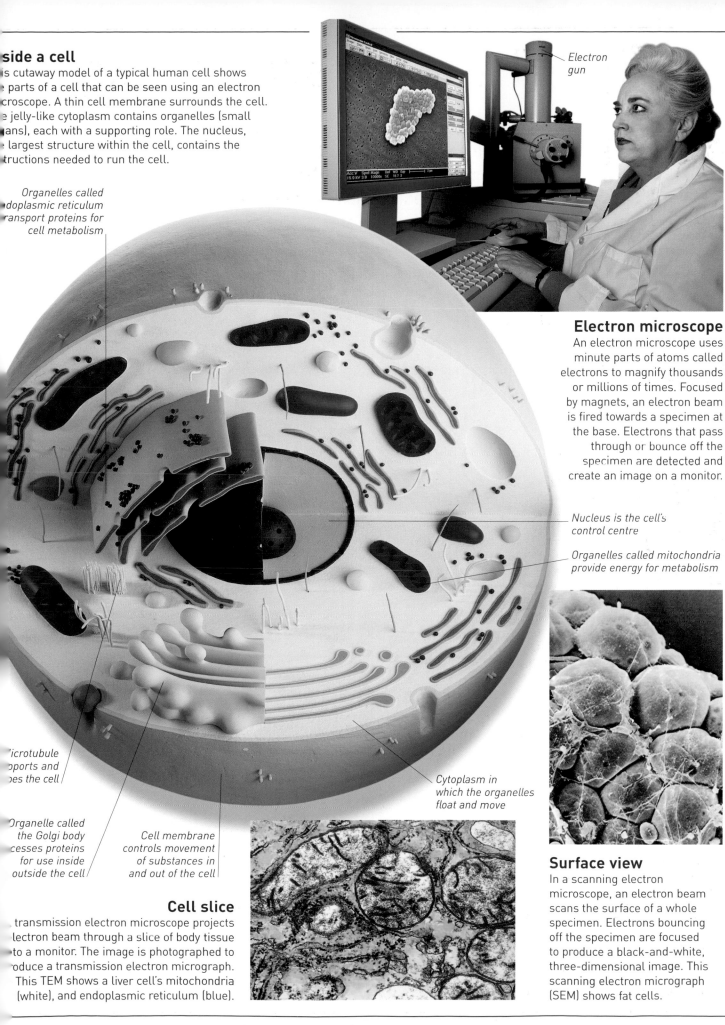

side a cell

is cutaway model of a typical human cell shows
parts of a cell that can be seen using an electron
croscope. A thin cell membrane surrounds the cell.
e jelly-like cytoplasm contains organelles (small
ans), each with a supporting role. The nucleus,
largest structure within the cell, contains the
tructions needed to run the cell.

*Organelles called
doplasmic reticulum
ransport proteins for
cell metabolism*

*Electron
gun*

Electron microscope

An electron microscope uses
minute parts of atoms called
electrons to magnify thousands
or millions of times. Focused
by magnets, an electron beam
is fired towards a specimen at
the base. Electrons that pass
through or bounce off the
specimen are detected and
create an image on a monitor.

*Nucleus is the cell's
control centre*

*Organelles called mitochondria
provide energy for metabolism*

*icrotubule
ports and
es the cell*

*Cytoplasm in
which the organelles
float and move*

*Organelle called
the Golgi body
cesses proteins
for use inside
outside the cell*

*Cell membrane
controls movement
of substances in
and out of the cell*

Surface view

In a scanning electron
microscope, an electron beam
scans the surface of a whole
specimen. Electrons bouncing
off the specimen are focused
to produce a black-and-white,
three-dimensional image. This
scanning electron micrograph
(SEM) shows fat cells.

Cell slice

transmission electron microscope projects
lectron beam through a slice of body tissue
to a monitor. The image is photographed to
oduce a transmission electron micrograph.
This TEM shows a liver cell's mitochondria
(white), and endoplasmic reticulum (blue).

Looking inside the body

In the past, the only way to see inside the body was to cut it open or inspect soldiers' wounds. The invention of the ophthalmoscope in 1851 allowed doctors to view the inside of a patient's eye for the first time. In 1895, X-rays were discovered and used to produce images of bones without cutting open the body. Today's imaging techniques allow us to view tissues, search for signs of disease, and find out how the body works.

War wounds
This illustration from a German medical manual of 1540 shows surgeons how to extract an arrowhead from a soldier on the battlefield.

Screw widens nose-piece to hold open nostril

Screws onto the otoscope here

Nasal speculum for examining the nose

Angled mirror to reflect the view

Rotating set of magnifying lenses for examining the eye

Mirror head for the laryngoscope

Tongue-depressor for the laryngoscope

Finger bones are clearly visible

Light source in the tip

Funnel-shaped tip inserted into the outer ear canal

Head attachments screw on here

Metal rings and key chain

Handle

Mysterious rays
This radiograph from 1896 was produced by projecting X-rays (a form of radiation) through a woman's hand onto a photographic plate. Hard bones and metal show up clearly since they absorb X-rays that pass through softer tissues.

Otoscope head for examining inside the ear

Laryngoscope head for examining the throat

CT scanning
A computed tomography (CT) scan uses X-rays and a computer to look inside the body. A patient lies inside a rotating scanner, which sends a narrow beam of X-rays through the body to a detector. The result is a two-dimensional slice of the body showing hard and soft tissues. A computer combines image slices together to build up a three-dimensional picture of a body part, such as this living heart.

Medical viewing kit
Today's doctors routinely use this multipurpose medical equipment when examining patients in the surgery. The kit consists of a handle, which contains batteries to power a light source, and a range of attachments used for looking inside the ears, throat, nose, or eyes. For example, using the ophthalmoscope attachment, a doctor can shine a light and look into a patient's eye.

Opthalmoscope

Inside of body visible on the monitor

Surgeon moves the endoscope to a new position

Endoscope

Surgeons use a thin, tube-like endoscope to examine tissues and to look inside joints. It is inserted via a natural body opening, such as the mouth, or a small incision in the skin (as shown here). Optical fibres inside the tube carry bright light to illuminate the inside of the body and send back images to a monitor.

Magnets and radio waves

Inside a magnetic resonance imaging (MRI) scanner, a powerful magnetic field lines up the hydrogen atoms in the patient's body. Bursts of radio waves knock the atoms back into position. When the magnetic field lines the atoms up again, they send out tiny radio signals. Different tissues and organs send out differing signals that are detected and turned into images by a computer.

Seeing

Hearing

Speaking

Thinking and speaking

ain tissue at work

itron emission tomography (PET) scans reveal active specific body tissues are. First, a form lucose (sugar) is injected into the bloodstream rovide food energy for hard-working tissues. he tissues consume the glucose, particles are ased that can be detected to form an image.

Brain inside the skull

Left lung inside the chest

Full body scan

This MRI scan shows a vertical cross-section through a man's body. This is produced by combining many individual scans made along the length of the body. The original black and white image has been colour enhanced to highlight different tissues and organs.

ht hand ing next to head

Side view of fetus's head

Urinary bladder in the lower abdomen

Femur (thigh bone) extends from the hip to the knee

Fleshy calf muscle in the lower leg

m echo to image

sound scanning produces moving images such is fetus inside the womb. High-pitched sound s are beamed into the body, reflected back by es, and converted into images by a computer.

Video pill

This capsule endoscope can be used to identify damage or disease in the digestive system. It contains a tiny camera, light source, and transmitter. Once swallowed, it travels along the digestive system, taking pictures that are then transmitted to an outside receiver for a doctor to view.

The body's framework

The skeleton's 206 bones make up a hard yet flexible framework that serves to support and shape the body. It surrounds and protects organs such as the brain and heart, and stops them being jolted or crushed. Bones als[o] provide anchorage for the muscles that move the skeleto[n] and, therefore, the whole body. Unlike early anatomists, today's scientists can examine bones inside a living body.

Symbol of death
Skeletons are enduring symbols of danger, disease, death, and destruction – as seen in this 15th-century *Dance of Death* drawing.

Understanding bones
For centuries, bones were regarded as lifeless supports for the active, softer tissues around them. Gradually, anatomists saw that bones were alive, with their own blood vessels and nerves. Here, the renowned medieval surgeon Guy de Chauliac, author of *Great Surgery* (1363), examines a fracture, or broken bone.

Body mechanics
Many machines copy principles of mechanics shown by the skeleton. For example, each arm has two sets of long bones that can extend the reach of the hand, or fold back on themselves – like these cranes.

Spinal cord is protected by the vertebrae

Model backbone
The backbone, or spine, is a strong, flexible colum[n] of 33 vertebrae that keeps the body upright. Each vertebra has a centrum, which bears the body's weight. A pad of cartilage forms a cushion betwee[n] one centrum and the next. This allows limited movement between neighbouring vertebrae. All these tiny movements added together along the length of the backbone enable the body to ben[d] forwards, backwards, side to side, and to twist.

Spino[us] proce[ss]

Cen[trum]

Early 19th-century drawi[ng] of a lumbar vertebra, seen from above

Centrum (body) of the vertebra

Intervertebral disc of cartilage

Lumbar (lower back) section of the spine

Spinous process (bump) for muscle attachment

Metatarsals (sole bones)

Tarsals (ankle bones)

Talus connects to [the] (shin bone) and fib[ula]

Calcaneus (heel bone)

Phalanges (toe bones) of smaller toe

Phalanges of big toe

Bones of the f[eet]
The feet bear the whole weight of the body and each o[f] made up of 26 bones: seven in the ankle, five in the sole, three in each toe, apart from the big toe which has

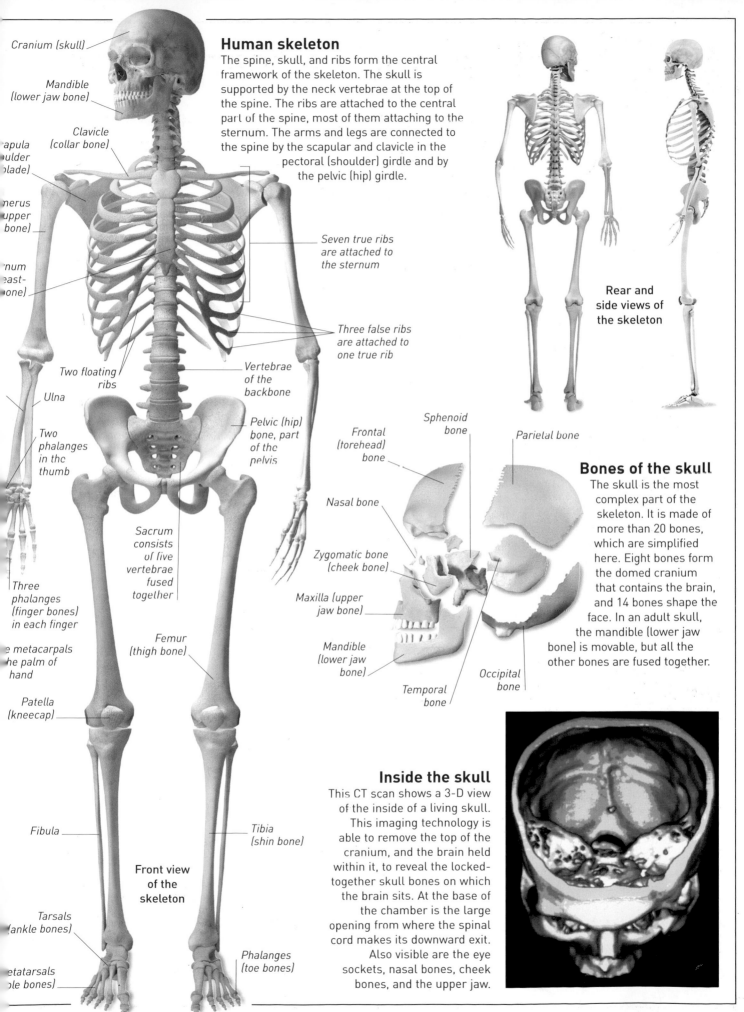

Cranium (skull)

Mandible (lower jaw bone)

Clavicle (collar bone)

...apula ...ulder ...lade)

...nerus ...upper ...bone)

...num ...east- ...one)

Two floating ribs

Ulna

Two phalanges in the thumb

Three phalanges (finger bones) in each finger

...e metacarpals ...he palm of ...hand

Patella (kneecap)

Fibula

Tarsals (ankle bones)

...etatarsals ...le bones)

Human skeleton

The spine, skull, and ribs form the central framework of the skeleton. The skull is supported by the neck vertebrae at the top of the spine. The ribs are attached to the central part of the spine, most of them attaching to the sternum. The arms and legs are connected to the spine by the scapular and clavicle in the pectoral (shoulder) girdle and by the pelvic (hip) girdle.

Seven true ribs are attached to the sternum

Three false ribs are attached to one true rib

Vertebrae of the backbone

Pelvic (hip) bone, part of the pelvis

Sacrum consists of five vertebrae fused together

Femur (thigh bone)

Tibia (shin bone)

Front view of the skeleton

Phalanges (toe bones)

Rear and side views of the skeleton

Sphenoid bone

Frontal (forehead) bone

Parietal bone

Nasal bone

Zygomatic bone (cheek bone)

Maxilla (upper jaw bone)

Mandible (lower jaw bone)

Temporal bone

Occipital bone

Bones of the skull

The skull is the most complex part of the skeleton. It is made of more than 20 bones, which are simplified here. Eight bones form the domed cranium that contains the brain, and 14 bones shape the face. In an adult skull, the mandible (lower jaw bone) is movable, but all the other bones are fused together.

Inside the skull

This CT scan shows a 3-D view of the inside of a living skull. This imaging technology is able to remove the top of the cranium, and the brain held within it, to reveal the locked-together skull bones on which the brain sits. At the base of the chamber is the large opening from where the spinal cord makes its downward exit. Also visible are the eye sockets, nasal bones, cheek bones, and the upper jaw.

Inside bones

Our bones are living organs with a complex structure of hard bone tissues, blood vessels, and nerves. Bone is as strong as steel, but only one-sixth its weight. Each bone also has a slight springiness that enables it to withstand knocks and jolts, usual without breaking. Tough, dense bony tissue, called compact bone, surrounds light-but-strong spongy bone inside – otherwi the skeleton would be too heavy for the body to move.

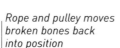

Growing bone
In a young embryo the skeleton forms from bendy cartilage, which then turns into bone over time. This X-ray of a young child's hand shows growing bones (dark blue) and spaces where cartilage will be replaced.

Rope and pulley moves broken bones back into position

Setting bones
Skeletons of 100,000 years ago show that broken bones were set, or repositioned, to aid healing. Here, 17th-century surgeons are setting a broken arm.

Resisting pressure
When weight is put on a bone, its structure prevents it from bending. For example, in the hip joint (shown here in cross-section) the head and neck of the femur (thigh bone) bear the full weight of the body. The largest area of bone consists of spongy bone, in which the trabeculae, or framework of struts, are lined up to resist downward force. The thin covering of compact bone resists squashing on one side of the femur and stretching on the opposite side.

Pelvic (hip) bone

Head and neck of the femur (thigh bone)

Spongy bone

Compact bone resists squashing

Compact bone resists stretching

Mu

Inside a long bone
In the cutaway below, compact bone forms the hard outer layer. It is made up of parallel bundles of osteons (see opposite) that run lengthways and act as weight-bearing pillars. Inside is lighter spongy bone and a central, marrow-filled cavity.

Spongy bone
This SEM of spongy, or cancellous, bone shows an open framework of struts and spaces, or trabeculae. In living bone these form a structure of great strength and the spaces are filled with bone marrow. Spongy bone is lighter than compact bone, and so reduces the overall weight of a bone.

Head of bone is mostly spongy bone

Artery supplies oxygen-rich blood to the bone cells

Bone expert

Italy's Giovanni Ingrassias (1510–80) was a founder of osteology, or the study of bones. His research corrected many mistaken ideas about bones. Ingrassias also identified the body's smallest bone, the stapes (stirrup) of the ear, and he described the arrangement of skull bones that form part of the eye socket.

Osteon

Lamellae (layered tubes) of the osteon

Blood vessel

Outer lamellae strengthen the whole bone

Osteocyte (bone cell)

Bone cells

This SEM shows an osteocyte (bone cell) in a lacuna – a tiny space in the framework of minerals and fibres that makes up compact bone. Osteocytes are linked by strand-like extensions of their cell bodies that pass along the narrow canals inside bone.

ne micro-structure

s model shows a microscopic view
slice of compact bone, made up
ayered osteons measuring just
5 mm (0.01 in) across. Blood
sels run through their central
al, supplying food and
gen to the bone cells to
intain the bone framework.
s is made of bendy fibres
he protein collagen and
d minerals, mainly calcium
osphate, which make the
e strong but not brittle.

Periosteum

Central canal of the osteon

Branch of blood vessel between the osteons

Spongy bone

ne marrow

y-like bone marrow fills the spaces
de spongy bone and the central cavity
ong bones. As the body grows, bone-cell-
king red marrow is gradually replaced by
storing yellow marrow. In adults, red bone
rrow remains only in a few bones, such as
skull, spine, and breastbone. These sites
ase more than two million red blood cells
second into the bloodstream.

Periosteum, a thin, fibrous membrane covering the bone

Head of bone

Rich network of blood vessels nourishes the bone

Compact bone is the hard, dense outer layer of the bone

Bone shaft

Osteon is one of the layered tubes that make up compact bone

Central cavity

Vein carries oxygen-poor blood away from the bone cells

Yellow bone marrow fills the central cavity and stores fat

Making new blood cells

This SEM shows red bone marrow, where blood cells are made. Unspecialized stem cells multiply to produce cells that rapidly multiply again to form billions of red blood cells (red) and white blood cells (blue).

The body's joints

Wherever two or more bones meet in the skeleton, they form a joint. Most of the body's 400-plus joints, such as those in our fingers and toes, are synovial, or freely movable. There are several types of movable joint, held together by ligaments, which makes the skeleton incredibly flexible. Without them, it would be rigid.

Pivot jo[int] allows [the] head to shake

Condyloid joint allows the head to nod

Hinge joint allows the arm to bend at the elbow

Supple joints
Joints benefit from use, and deteriorate with neglect. Activities such as yoga promote the full range of joint movement and enjoy maximum flexibility.

Simple hinge joints between the phalanges (finger bones) enable the fingers to bend in two places

Condyloid joint is an oval ball-and-socket joint allowing the fingers to swivel, but not to rotate

Palm of hand extends to the knuckles

Gliding joints allow limited sliding movements between the eight bones of the wrist

Saddle joint gives thumb great flexibility and a delicate touch when picking up tiny objects with the fingers

Limb can move in many directions

Femur (thigh bone)

Pelvic (hip) bone

Ball-and-socket joint in the hip

Balls, sockets, and hinges
The hip and knee's movements can be seen whenever someone climbs, walks, dances, or kicks. The hip joint is a ball-and-socket joint. The rounded end of the thigh bone swivels in the cup-shaped socket in the hip bone and permits movement in all directions, including rotation. The knee is a hinge joint and moves mainly in one front-to-back direction.

Femur (thigh bone)

Tibia (shin bone)

Hinge joint in the knee

Limb moves back and forth in one direction

Gliding joint allows the kneecap to move away from the femur (thigh bone) as the knee bend[s]

Hinge joint allow[s] the foot to bend [at] the ankle

Joints galore
With its 27 bones and 19 movable joints, the hand can perform many delicate tasks. The first knuckle joint of each digit (finger) is condyloid – it and the other hinge joints allow the fingers to curl around and grasp objects. The saddle joint at the base of the thumb – the most mobile digit – allows it to swing across the palm and touch the tips of the other fingers for a precise grip.

Versatile mover
The skeleton is extremely flexible because it contains many different types of joint, each permitting different ranges of movement. Ball-and-socket, condyloid, and saddle joints allow flexible movements in several directions. Others are more limited. Pivot joints allow movement from side to side, hinge joints back and forth, and gliding joints enable small sliding movements between bones.

Binding the bones
Tough straps of strong, elastic tissue called ligaments surround bone ends in a joint – such as the ankle – and bind them together securely to prevent them from moving excessively.

Tibia (shin bone)

Fibula

Ligament linking the calcaneus and fibula

Calcaneus (heel bone)

Pivot joint permits the forearm to twist

Gliding joint between the rib and backbone

Saddle joint gives the thumb great mobility

Condyloid joint gives the wrist flexibility

Metatarsals (sole bones)

Ligament linking the tibia and fibula

Tarsal (ankle bone)

Ligaments connecting the tarsals and metatarsals

Inside a synovial joint
This view into a typical, movable joint shows its main parts. Inside the protective joint capsule and ligaments is the synovial membrane. This makes synovial fluid, the oil that lubricates the joint. The bone ends are covered by friction-reducing, shiny hyaline cartilage.

Bone marrow

Bone

Joint capsule

Synovial fluid

Synovial membrane

Hyaline cartilage

Ligaments

Cartilage
Tough and flexible, cartilage is a supporting tissue that resists pushing and pulling forces. There are three types. Hyaline cartilage covers bone ends to help joints move smoothly. It also, amongst other things, connects the ribs to the sternum. Elastic cartilage is strong and stretchy. It supports the outside of the ear, for example. Fibrocartilage can withstand heavy pressure and is found in the discs between vertebrae in the backbone and in the knee joints.

Ball-and-socket joint between the femur (thigh bone) and hip enables the leg to move in all directions

Hinge joint allows the leg to bend at the knee

Gliding joint between the tarsals (ankle bones) allows little movement, which strengthens the ankle

Condyloid joint allows the toes to bend and wiggle

Hinge joint allows the toe to bend

Cartilage cells
Cells called chondrocytes make cartilage around themselves. It consists of two types of fibres – the tough protein collagen and the elastic protein elastin, woven together into a stiff jelly with water. Nutrients seep into cartilage cells from the blood vessels that run around its edges.

Chondrocyte

Knee trouble
The knee is the body's biggest joint. It is strengthened by ligaments inside the joint, and cushioned from jolts by pads of cartilage called the menisci. Sports such as football involve rapid turns and high kicks, which can cause knee injuries.

Muscle power

Muscle tissue pulls – and generates movement – by contracting, or getting shorter. Skeletal muscles make up nearly half the body's total mass. They shape the body and, by pulling on bones, hold it upright to maintain posture and allow it to perform a wide range of movements from blinking to running. The two other muscle types are smooth and cardiac muscle. Most muscles have Latin names that describe their location, size, shape, or action.

Under the microscope
Danish scientist and bishop Nicholas Steno (1638–86) looked at muscle with a microscope and found that their contraction was due to the combined shortening of the thousands of tiny fibres that make up each muscle.

The ultimate book
Italian anatomist Giorgio Baglivi (1668–1707) was the first to note that skeletal muscles differ from the muscles working the intestines and other organs.

Trapezius acts to brace the shoulders and pull back the head

Latissimus dorsi pulls the arm backwards and downwards

Deltoid raises the arm away from the body, to the side, front, or rear

Semispinalis capitis tilts the head to look up

Infraspinatus rotates the arm outwards

Myofibril

Bundle of muscle fibres

Muscle fibre

Motor neuron (nerve cell)

Epimysium

Sternocleidomastoid tilts the head

Pectoralis major pulls the arm in and rotates it

Inside a skeletal muscle
Skeletal muscles are made from long, cylindrical cells called muscle fibres. Each fibre is packed with parallel, rod-like myofibrils that cause contraction. Bundles of fibres are wrapped inside a tough sheath, the epimysium, to form a muscle. Motor neurons (nerve cells) carry signals from the brain, which tell the muscle fibres to contract.

Biceps

Masseter closes an open jaw

Pectoralis minor pulls the shoulder downwards

Intercostal muscles move the ribs in breathing

Gluteus maximus straightens the hip

Biceps femoris, one of the hamstrings, bends the knee

Gastrocnemius lifts the heel and bends the knee

Calcaneal (Achilles) tendon, the body's biggest, attaches the calf muscles to the heel bone

Tibialis posterior counteracts sway when standing on one foot

Flexor hallucis longus curls the sole and toes downwards

Rear view

Gluteus minimus pulls the thigh out to the side

...side of the navel tense to hold in a flabby belly

Flexor carpi radialis bends the wrist

Sartorius twists the thigh and bends the hip and knee

Muscle types

Skeletal muscle moves the bones. Seen under a microscope, its fibres appear striated (striped). It is a voluntary muscle, contracting when told to by the brain. Smooth muscle, with its sheets of tapering fibres, is found in the walls of hollow organs such as the intestines and lungs. This involuntary muscle works without the conscious involvement of the brain. Cardiac muscle, in the heart, contracts automatically and tirelessly for a lifetime.

Skeletal (striated) muscle

Smooth (involuntary) muscle

Cardiac (heart) muscle

Flexor digitorum longus bends the toes downwards to help the foot grip the ground

Deep muscles

If some superficial muscles are peeled away, deeper muscles are exposed – as shown on the left half of these bodies. Many of these muscles lie directly next to the bones they pull, and the points where they join may be visible.

Superficial muscles

The body has more than 640 skeletal muscles, criss-crossing and overlapping, so that each bone may be pulled in almost any direction. Muscles just under the skin's surface are called superficial muscles – as shown on the right half of these two bodies.

Tibialis anterior raises the foot

Internal oblique bends and rotates the trunk

Adductor longus pulls the leg towards the centre of the body

Quadriceps femoris straightens the knee

Extensor digitorum longus curls the toes upwards and raises the ball of the foot

Front view

23

The moving body

Muscles are attached to bones by tough, fibrous cords called tendons. When muscles contract (get shorter), the pull on a bone. The bone that moves when the muscle contracts is called the insertion and the other bone, whic stays still, is called the origin. Muscles can only pull, not push, so moving a body part in different directions requires opposing pairs of muscles.

The three S-words
Muscle fitness can be assessed by strength, stamina, and suppleness. Swimming and dancing promote all three.

Extensor tendon to the index finger

Phalanges (finger bones)

Transverse ligament stops the tendons moving sideways

Muscles in the back of the forearm extend (straighten) the fingers

Neck muscles bend the head bac

Biceps contracted

Triceps relaxed

Triceps contracted

Back muscles arch the back

Raised forearm

Flexed elbow

Biceps relaxed

Extensor retinaculum holds the long tendons in place

Separate extensor tendons begin at the end of the extensor digitorum

Elbow straight

Extensor digitorum straightens the fingers when it contracts

Forearm lowered

Muscle pairs
Muscles can only contract and pull, so moving a body part in opposite directions requires two different muscles. Many muscles are arranged in opposing pairs. In the arm, the biceps pulls the forearm upwards and bends the elbow, while its opposing partner, the triceps, pulls the forearm downwards and straightens the elbow.

Tendons
Many of the muscles that move the fingers are not in the hand, but in the forearm. They work the fingers by remote control, using long tendons extending from the ends of the muscles to attach to the bones that they move. The tendons run smoothly in slippery tendon sheaths that reduce wear.

Power and precision
With practice, pianists can tr their brains to coordinate complex, rhythmic movemen all ten fingers. Muscles work flexible framework of 27 bon each hand to play notes rang from delicate to explosive.

orking together

[To] perform the pose below, areas of the brain [th]at control movement and balance send out [ner]ve signals to instruct specific skeletal [mu]scles when to contract and by how much. [Mu]scles in the hands, arms, torso, and legs [wo]rk together to put the gymnast in this [po]sition. Signals from the muscles and [ten]dons also feed back to the brain so that [mi]nor adjustments maintain her balance.

Calf muscles bend the foot downwards to point the toes

[H]and muscles pull [the] fingers together

Muscles at the back of the thigh pull the leg backwards

[M]uscle at [th]e front of [th]e thigh [p]ulls the [f]orwards and [str]aightens [t]he knee

[P]airs of [mu]scles at [th]e front [and] back of the leg [t]ense to keep [b]alance

Old theories
Dutch physician Jan Swammerdam (1637–90) disproved ideas that a vital spirit passed along nerves and inflated muscles to make them contract. He showed that muscles altered in shape, but not in volume (the space they take up) during contraction.

Myofibril contraction
This TEM shows myofibrils, the long cylinders that extend the length of a skeletal muscle fibre, or cell. Here, running from left to right, they are divided into units between the thin, vertical lines. Each unit contains thick and thin filaments, producing the blue-and-pink pattern. The thick and thin filaments slide over each other, making the myofibril – and the entire muscle – shorter.

Frontalis raises the eyebrows and wrinkles the forehead

Orbicularis oculi closes the eye

Corrugator supercilii pulls the eyebrows together

Levator labii superioris lifts and curls the upper lip

Orbicularis oris closes, purses, and protrudes the lips – during a kiss, for example

Mentalis protrudes the lower lip

Depressor anguli oris pulls down the corner of the mouth

Temporalis lifts the lower jaw, during biting, for example

Face, head, and neck
From frowning to smiling, around 30 facial muscles produce the great variety of expressions. These muscles are also involved in activities such as blinking and chewing. They work by joining the skull bones to different areas of skin, which are tugged as the muscles contract. The head is supported and moved by muscles that start at the backbone, shoulder blades, and bones in the upper chest.

Zygomatic muscles raise the corners of the mouth upwards

Risorius pulls the corner of the mouth in a smile

Sternocleidomastoid tilts the head forward or to one side

Trapezius pulls the head upright

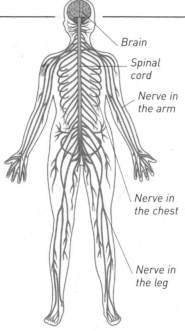

Brain

Spinal cord

Nerve in the arm

Nerve in the chest

Nerve in the leg

Nerve network
The brain and spinal cord form the control centre of a network of nerves. Nerves are bundles of interconnected neuron cells, and divide to reach all of the body's tissues. Laid end to end, a body's nerves would circle Earth twice.

The nervous system

Without the control and coordination of its nervous system, the body could not function. With split-second timing, our nervous system allows us to feel, see, and hear, to move, and to think and remember – all at the same time. It also automatically controls many internal body processes. It is run by the brain and spinal cord, which form the central nervous system (CNS) and link to the body's network of nerves.

Facial nerve controls the muscles of facial expression

Trigeminal nerve branch supplies the upper teeth and cheek

Brachial plexus leads to the nerves that supply the arm and hand

Ulnar nerve controls the muscles that bend the wrist and fingers

Intercostal nerve controls the muscles between the ribs

Pavlov's performing dogs
A reflex is an automatic reaction to a particular stimulus, or trigger. Dogs naturally salivate (drool) at the sight and smell of food. Russian scientist Ivan Pavlov (1849–1936) trained some dogs to associate feeding time with the sound of a bell. In time, they drooled when hearing the bell alone.

Cranial and spinal nerves
The brain – the cerebrum, cerebellum, and brain stem – and the spinal cord function through a constant flow of signals. These arrive and depart through 12 pairs of cranial nerves that start in the brain, and 31 pairs of spinal nerves that start in the spinal cord. Each nerve has sensory neurons, which carry sensations from a body area to the brain, and motor neurons, which carry instructions from the brain to move muscles in that same area. Part of the nervous system automatically controls vital processes that we are unaware of, such as the body's heart rate.

Branches everywhere
These are association neurons in the brain. Each has branching links with thousands of other neurons, forming a communication network with countless routes for nerve signals travelling beween neurons.

Cerebrum processes
and stores information

Cerebellum
controls
movement
and balance

Brain stem
controls the heart
rate and breathing

Spinal cord
relays signals
between the
spinal nerves
and the brain

Sympathetic
ganglion chain
controls automatic
functions

Spinal nerves
are arranged
in pairs

Phrenic nerve
supplies the
diaphragm,
the muscle that
causes breathing

Axon bundle
carries signals to
and from the brain

Spinal nerve

Front root carries
outgoing signals

Back root carries
incoming signals

Grey matter
contains
neuron cell
bodies

White matter
consists of
axon bundles

Meninges
are three
protective
membranes

Founder of neurology

French physician Jean-Martin
Charcot (1825–93) was a
pioneer of neurology, the study
of nervous system diseases,
and of psychiatry, the branch
of medicine that deals with
mental illness.

Cross-section of the spinal cord

The spinal cord relays nerve signals between
the spinal nerves and the brain. Each spinal
nerve has two roots. One contains sensory
neurons bringing incoming signals from sense
receptors. The other contains motor neurons
carrying outgoing signals to the muscles. The
spinal cord also controls many automatic body
reflexes, such as pulling the hand away from a
hot or sharp object.

Neuron structure

A neuron is a nerve cell body
with many short, branched
endings called dendrites and
one long axon, or nerve fibre.
Dendrites receive nerve signals
from other neurons across
junctions called synapses.
Axons carry nerve signals
away from the cell body,
across synapses with other
neurons or with muscles.

Vagus nerve
helps control
the heart rate

Part of
another
neuron

Neuron's cell
body contains
its nucleus

Synapse
between
two
neurons

Dendrite

Axon
(nerve fibre)

Longest axon
is up to 1 m
(3 ft) long

Insulating
myelin sheath
increases
speed of
signals

The brain

The brain is our most complex organ and our nervous system's control centre. It contains 100 billion neurons (nerve cells), each linked to hundreds or thousands of other neurons, which together form a vast communication network with incredible processing power. Over the past two centuries, scientists have mapped the brain and how it works.

Metal rod

Hole in the head

Phineas Gage worked in a quarry in the USA. In 1848, a gunpowder accident blew a metal rod through the left frontal lobe of his brain. Gage survived, but he changed from contented and polite to moody, and foul-mouthed – living proof that the front of the brain is involved in persona

The brain from below

The brain has three main parts. The cerebrum dominates the brain and makes up 85 per cent of its weight. It processes and stores incoming information and sends out instructions to the body. The brain stem relays signals between the cerebrum and the spinal cord, and controls automatic functions, such as the heart rate and breathing. The cerebellum is responsible for controlling balance and posture and for coordinating movements.

Left hemisphere of cerebrum controls right side of the bod

Olfactory bul carries signa from the nose the brain

Optic ne (shown carries signals the eyes the bran

Pons is the middle part of the brain stem

Medu oblor is pa the b stem contr brea and t hear

Cerebellum co body movemen

Right hemisphere of the cerebrum controls the left side of the body

Spinal cord (shown cu relays signals betwee the brain and body

Left and right

The right hemisphere (half) of the cerebrum receives sensory input from, and controls the movements of, the left side of the body, and vice versa. The right side of the brain also handles face recognition, and creative abilities such as music, while the left side controls language, problem solving, and mathematical skills. Left-handed people, such as rock guitarist Jimi Hendrix (1942–70), often excel in the creative arts and music.

Premotor cortex controls complex movements

Primary motor cortex controls muscles

Primary sensory cortex receives input from skin

Sensory association cortex interprets touch signals

Visual association cortex interprets images

Prefrontal cortex controls reasoning and learning

Broca's area controls speech

Primary auditory cortex receives input from ears

Auditory association cortex interprets sounds

Primary visual cortex receives input from eyes

Wernicke's area interprets language

Brain map

Different areas of the cerebral cortex carry out specific tasks, as shown in this map of the left hemisphere. Sensory areas of the cortex deal with input from the sensory detectors. Motor areas of the cortex control the body's movement. Most of the cortex is made up of association areas, which interpret and analyse information used in learning and memory.

e of speech

ch physician Paul Pierre
a (1824–80) had a patient
a limited ability to speak.
the patient died, Broca
d a damaged patch on his
cerebrum. He realized this
coordinated the muscles
e larynx and mouth that
used for speaking.

rontal lobe
he front of
e cerebral
emisphere

eft cerebral
emisphere

mporal lobe
the side of
he cerebral
emisphere

etal lobe on
the rear top
section of
the cerebral
emisphere

ital lobe at the
of the cerebral
hemisphere

Longitudinal fissure separates the two cerebral hemispheres

Blood supply

This angiogram shows the brain's blood supply. The brain makes up only two per cent of the body's weight, but receives 20 per cent of the body's total blood supply. This delivers the oxygen and glucose (sugar) that the brain requires to function normally.

Gyrus (ridge)

Right cerebral hemisphere

Sulcus (groove)

The brain from above

The surface layer of the cerebrum, called the cerebral cortex, is heavily folded with ridges and grooves. These greatly increase the surface area of cerebral cortex that can fit inside the skull. If laid out flat, the cortex would cover about the same area as a pillow. Deep grooves divide each hemisphere into four areas, called the frontal, temporal, parietal, and occipital lobes.

Inside the brain

Deep inside the brain, under the cerebrum, the thalamus acts as a relay station for incoming nerve signals, and the hypothalamus automatically controls a vast array of body activities. The limbic system is the emotional centre of the brain, dealing with instincts, fears, and feelings. Inside the cerebrum, linked chambers called ventricles are filled with cerebrospinal fluid (CSF). CSF is produced by blood and circulates through the ventricles, helping to feed the brain cells.

Liquid brainpower

Long ago, a mystical animal spirit was said to fill the brain's ventricles. This 17th-century image links each ventricle to a different mental quality, such as imagination.

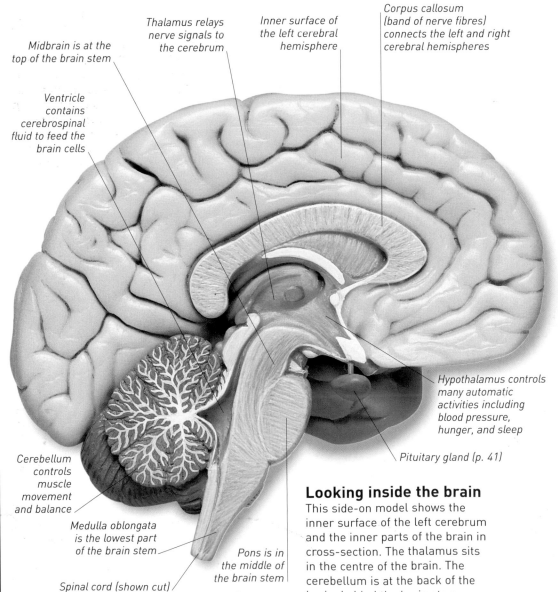

Midbrain is at the top of the brain stem

Thalamus relays nerve signals to the cerebrum

Inner surface of the left cerebral hemisphere

Corpus callosum (band of nerve fibres) connects the left and right cerebral hemispheres

Ventricle contains cerebrospinal fluid to feed the brain cells

Hypothalamus controls many automatic activities including blood pressure, hunger, and sleep

Cerebellum controls muscle movement and balance

Medulla oblongata is the lowest part of the brain stem

Pons is in the middle of the brain stem

Spinal cord (shown cut)

Pituitary gland (p. 41)

Looking inside the brain

This side-on model shows the inner surface of the left cerebrum and the inner parts of the brain in cross-section. The thalamus sits in the centre of the brain. The cerebellum is at the back of the brain, behind the brain stem.

Matters of the m

Austrian physician Sigmund F (1856–1939) used psychoanalys treat mental illness by investig the unconscious mind. Since F pyschiatrists have linked m disorders to abnormaliti the brain's structure ar biochemical work

Support c

Over 90 per cent of cells nervous system are not ne (nerve cells) but glial, or su cells. Astrocytes, a type of glia found in the cerebral cortex to supply neurons with nutr Other functions of glia include destroying bacter insulating axons (nerve f

Cingulate gyrus deals with emotions

Fornix is the pathway that links different parts of the limbic system

The limbic system

A curve of linked structures is located on the inner surface of each cerebral hemisphere and around the top of the brain stem. It deals with emotions such as pleasure, anger, fear, hope, and sadness, and helps us to store memories. As the sense of smell is linked to the limbic system, certain odours can trigger feelings and memories.

Olfactory bulb carries signals from the smell receptors in the nose directly to the limbic system

Mamillary body relays signals from the amygdala and hippocampus to the thalamus

Hippocampus deals with memory and navigation

Parahippocampal gyrus deals with anger and fright, and recalls memories

Amygdala assesses danger and triggers feelings of fear

ep thought

nch sculptor Auguste Rodin
0–1917) portrayed deep
centration in his statue *The*
ker. When we want to think
d about a matter, we stare
space, almost unseeing,
hat we can concentrate.

Sweet dreams

French artist Henri Rousseau (1844–1910) painted a musician dreaming about a lion in *The Sleeping Gypsy*. In our dreams, real experiences can be mixed up with strange happenings. While we sleep, the brain replays recent experiences at random and stores significant events in the memory. Dreaming is a side effect of this activity.

White matter of cerebrum consists of axons encased in insulating sheaths

Cerebral cortex consists of grey matter

Longitudinal fissure separates the left and right cerebral hemispheres

Fornix is the nerve pathway that links parts of the limbic system

Corpus callosum (band of nerve fibres)

Thalamus relays incoming signals to the cerebral cortex

asal nuclei are o areas of grey er that control ody movement

Ventricle

Pons

y and te matter

vertical cross-
on gives a front
of the parts of the
rum. The cerebral
x – the surface layer
e brain – is made up of
matter. This consists of
n cell bodies, dendrites,
short axons. White matter
sts of longer axons, which
arts of the cerebral cortex
her, or connect the brain to
est of the nervous system.

Cerebellum

Spinal cord

Medulla oblongata

Mind over matter

Scientists continue to explore how the brain works. Some people look beyond its nerve signals and chemical processes, and believe that techniques such as meditation, performed here by a Buddhist monk, can carry the mind beyond the physical boundaries of the body.

Skin and touch

As well as its role in the sense of touch, skin has many other jobs. Its tough surface layer, the epidermis, keeps out water, dust, germs, and harmful ultraviolet rays from the Sun. Underneath is a thicker layer, the dermis, which is packed with sensory receptors, nerves, and blood vessels. It helps steady our body temperature at 37°C (98.6°F) by releasing sweat. Hair and nails provide additional body covering and protection.

Cooling the body
This is one of about three mill sweat pores in the skin's surfa When sweat glands in the der release sweat through the po the process draws heat from body and cools it down.

Fingertip reading
The Braille system enables people with sight problems to read using the sense of touch. It uses patterns of raised dots to represent letters and numbers, which are felt through the sensitive fingertips. The system was devised in 1824 by French teenager Louis Braille (1809–52), who was blinded at three years old.

Light touch and pressure receptor

Lowest layer of the epidermis replaces surface cells

Sebaceous gland releases sebum through the hair follicle

Tempe or pain recepto

Hair

Epidermis consists of several layers

Sweat pore

layer epid

Under your skin
The upper surface of the epidermis consists of dead cells filled with a tough protein, keratin. The skin flakes as dead cells wear away and are replaced with new ones produced in the lowest layer of the epidermis. The thicker dermis layer contains the sense receptors that help the body detect changes in temperature, touch, vibration, pressure, and pain. The dermis also houses coiled sweat glands and hair follicles. Oily sebum keeps the skin and hair soft and flexible.

Ridges on fingertips aid grip (see opposite)

Get a grip
The skin on the palm of the hand is covered with ridges. These help the hand to grip objects when performing different tasks. Beneath the palm, a triangle-shaped sheet of tough, meshed fibres anchors the skin and stops it from sliding over the underlying fat and muscle.

Lines on the palm of the hand

Nerve carries signals to the brain

Sweat gland

Loop pattern on fingerprint

~~Fin~~gerprints

~~The~~ skin on the fingers, toes, ~~palm~~s, and soles is folded into ~~swir~~ling patterns of tiny ridges. ~~The~~ ridges help this skin to ~~grip~~, aided by sweat released ~~thro~~ugh pores along each ~~ridg~~e. When fingers touch ~~smo~~oth surfaces, such as ~~glas~~s, their ridges leave behind ~~grea~~ty patterns, or prints, ~~feat~~uring arches, loops, and ~~swir~~ls. Each human has a ~~uniq~~ue set of fingerprints.

Nail grows from its root embedded in the skin

Nail body grows forwards over the nail bed

Nail bed is made up of deeper layers of the epidermis

Free edge of the nail can be trimmed

Skin

Tendon of muscle that bends the finger

Finger bone

Insensitive nails

Nails protect the ends of fingers and toes. They are hard extensions of the epidermis, made from dead cells filled with keratin. Each nail grows from new cells produced in the root. These push the nail body forwards over the nail bed as it grows.

Uncut fingernails curl as they grow

Nail growth

A typical fingernail grows about 3 mm (0.12 in) in a month. The nails on the longer fingers grow faster than those on the shorter ones. Fingernails also grow faster in the summer months than in winter. Toenails grow three or four times more slowly.

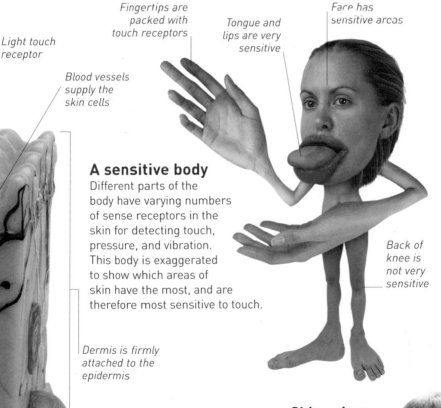

~~H~~air follicle ~~c~~ontains the ~~g~~rowing hair

Light touch receptor

Blood vessels supply the skin cells

Fingertips are packed with touch receptors

Tongue and lips are very sensitive

Face has sensitive areas

A sensitive body

Different parts of the body have varying numbers of sense receptors in the skin for detecting touch, pressure, and vibration. This body is exaggerated to show which areas of skin have the most, and are therefore most sensitive to touch.

Back of knee is not very sensitive

Dermis is firmly attached to the epidermis

Pressure and vibration receptor

Fat layer under the dermis insulates the body

Dead hairs

These hair shafts in the skin grow from living cells at the base of the follicle. As the cells push upwards, they fill with keratin and die. Short, fine hairs cover much of the body. Longer, thicker hairs protect the scalp from harmful sunlight and prevent heat loss.

Skin colour

Skin colour depends on how much melanin, or brown pigment (colouring), it contains. Melanin is produced by cells in the lowest layer of the epidermis. It protects against the harmful, ultraviolet rays in sunlight, which can damage skin cells and the tissues underneath. Sudden exposure of pale skin to strong sunlight can produce sunburn.

Eyes and seeing

The eyes contain over 70 per cent of the body's sensory receptors, in the form of light-detecting cells. Our eyes move automatically, adjust to dim and bright light, and focus light from objects near or far. This light is turned into electrical signals, sent to the brain, and changed into the images we see.

Cross-ey
This Arabic drawing, nea 1,000 years shows how optic nerves cross. Half c the nerve fik from the rig eye pass to the left side the brain, a vice versa.

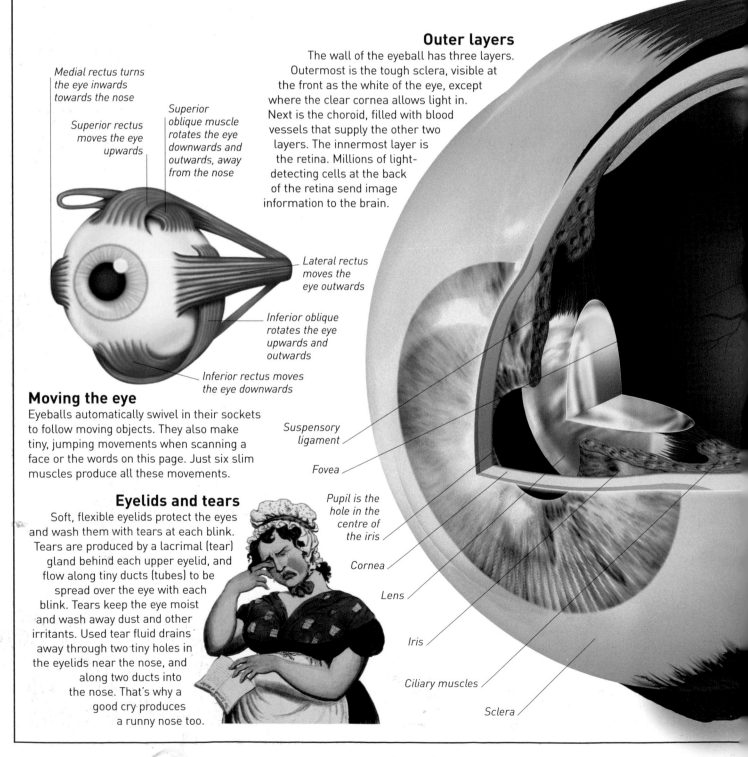

Outer layers

The wall of the eyeball has three layers. Outermost is the tough sclera, visible at the front as the white of the eye, except where the clear cornea allows light in. Next is the choroid, filled with blood vessels that supply the other two layers. The innermost layer is the retina. Millions of light-detecting cells at the back of the retina send image information to the brain.

Medial rectus turns the eye inwards towards the nose

Superior rectus moves the eye upwards

Superior oblique muscle rotates the eye downwards and outwards, away from the nose

Lateral rectus moves the eye outwards

Inferior oblique rotates the eye upwards and outwards

Inferior rectus moves the eye downwards

Moving the eye

Eyeballs automatically swivel in their sockets to follow moving objects. They also make tiny, jumping movements when scanning a face or the words on this page. Just six slim muscles produce all these movements.

Suspensory ligament

Fovea

Eyelids and tears

Soft, flexible eyelids protect the eyes and wash them with tears at each blink. Tears are produced by a lacrimal (tear) gland behind each upper eyelid, and flow along tiny ducts (tubes) to be spread over the eye with each blink. Tears keep the eye moist and wash away dust and other irritants. Used tear fluid drains away through two tiny holes in the eyelids near the nose, and along two ducts into the nose. That's why a good cry produces a runny nose too.

Pupil is the hole in the centre of the iris

Cornea

Lens

Iris

Ciliary muscles

Sclera

es forward

y one-sixth of an eyeball
be seen from the outside.
e rest sits protected within
eep bowl of skull bone,
eye socket. Eyebrows,
lids, and eyelashes
tect the front of the eye
shading it from dust,
eat, and excessive light.
e colour of the iris depends
the amount of the brown
ment melanin present.

*Eyelids protect
the eye from
bright light*

*Eyebrows direct
sweat away
from the eye*

*Tears drain away
through two ducts in
the corner of the eye*

*Pupil lets light
into the eye*

*Eyelashes protect
the eye from dust*

*Radial muscle
fibres relax*

Iris

*Circular muscle
fibres contract*

Pupil

Bright light

*Radial muscle
fibres contract*

Iris

*Circular
muscle
fibres relax*

Pupil

Dim light

Pupil size

Muscle fibres (red) in the iris adjust the size
of the pupil automatically. To avoid dazzle in
bright light, circular fibres contract to make
the pupil smaller. In dim light, to let more in,
radial fibres contract, to enlarge the pupil.

*Vitreous humour
within the body
of the eyeball*

*Blind spot is the
area that lacks
rods and cones*

*Optic nerve
carries nerve
signals from
the retina to
the brain*

Forming an image

When we look at an object, light rays reflected from
that object are partly focused, or bent, by the cornea.
The light then passes through the pupil to the lens,
which projects a sharp upside-down image onto the
retina. It sends nerve signals along the optic nerve to
the brain, which turns the image the right way up.

*Partial
focus by
the cornea*

*Fine-tune
focus by
the lens*

*Upside-down
image formed
at the back of
the retina*

*Light rays from the
object transmitted
to the eye*

*Lens shape is
adjusted by the
ciliary muscles*

*Optic
nerve*

Retina

Choroid

Rods and cones

The retina has two kinds
of light-detecting cells.
The rods (green) see only
in shades of grey, but
respond well in dim light.
The cones (blue) are
mainly at the back of the
retina and see details
and colours, but work
well only in bright light.

Inside the eye

Behind the cornea, the iris controls the
amount of light entering the eye through the
pil. The space behind the lens is filled with clear,
like vitreous humour. The most detailed images
roduced where light falls on the fovea, a part of
tina that contains only cones (see above, right).

Eye advances

German scientist Hermann von
Helmholtz (1821–94) studied the
mathematics of the eye in the *Handbook
of Physiological Optics*. He also helped
to invent the ophthalmoscope. Doctors
use this light-and-lens device for close-
up examinations of the eye's interior.

Ears and hearing

After sight, hearing provides the brain with the most information about the outside world. It enables us to work out the source, direction, and nature of sounds, and to communicate with each other. Our ears detect waves of pressure, called sound waves, which travel through the air from a vibrating sound source. The ears turn these waves into nerve signals, which the brain interprets as sounds that range from loud to quiet and from high pitched to low.

The mind's ear
German composer and pianist Ludwig van Beethoven (1770–1827) went deaf but continued to compose masterpieces by imagining the notes in his head.

Ear pioneer
The Examination of the Organ of Hearing, published in 1562, was probably the first major work devoted to ears. Its author was the Italian Bartolomeo Eustachio (c. 1520–74), a professor of anatomy in Rome. His name lives on in the Eustachian tube that he discovered, which connects the middle ear to the back of the throat.

Temporal bone of the skull

Scalp muscle

Cartilage supporting the pinna

The eardrum
The eardrum is a taut, delicate membrane, like the stretched skin on a drum, that vibrates when sound waves enter the ear. It separates the outer ear from the middle ear. Doctors can examine the eardrum through a medical instrument called an otoscope.

Hammer is one of three tiny bones behind the semi-transparent eardrum

Outer ear canal

Why ears pop
With equal air pressure on either side of the eardrum, it vibrates freely and so we hear clearly. A sudden change in pressure disrupts this. Yawning or swallowing opens the Eustachian tube and causes the ears to pop, as air moves into the middle ear and restores equal pressures.

Eustachian tube links the middle ear and throat

18th-century drawing of the ear

Inside the ear
Most of the ear lies inside the skull's temporal bone. It has three main parts. In the outer ear, the pinna (ear flap) directs sound waves into the ear canal. In the air-filled middle ear, behind the eardrum, three tiny bones called ossicles convert the sound waves into mechanical movement. The fluid-filled inner ear converts that movement into nerve signals.

Ear lobe of the pinna (ear flap)

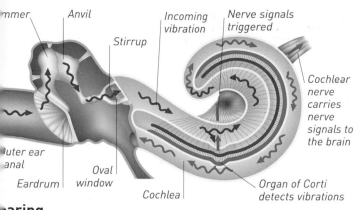

Hammer Anvil Incoming vibration Nerve signals triggered

Stirrup

Cochlear nerve carries nerve signals to the brain

Outer ear canal

Eardrum Oval window

Cochlea Organ of Corti detects vibrations

Incus (anvil) Stapedius muscle

Tensor tympani muscle

Malleus (hammer) Stapes (stirrup)

Smallest bones

The ossicles are tiny. The malleus (hammer) above is actual size. It is about 8 mm (0.3 in) long, almost twice the size of the stapes (stirrup).

Hearing

Sound waves funnelled into the ear canal strike the eardrum, making it vibrate. This makes the three ossicles move back and forth. The stirrup pushes and pulls the flexible oval window like a piston. This sets up vibrations in the fluid filling the cochlea. Inside the cochlea, sound-detecting hair cells turn the vibrations into nerve signals. These pass along the cochlear nerve to the hearing area of the brain.

Ossicles

The ossicles are the smallest bones in the body. They get their Latin names from their shapes. Attached to the bones are two of the body's smallest muscles. If a very loud sound reaches the eardrum, they contract to reduce the intense vibrations that would damage the inner ear.

The inner ear

The innermost part of the ear is made up of a maze of channels filled with fluid. One branch leads to the coiled cochlea. The vestibule houses the oval window – the membrane between the middle and inner ears – and two organs of balance, the utricle and saccule. Above the vestibule lies another balance organ, the semicircular canals.

Middle ear links the inner and outer ears

Semicircular canals

Vestibular nerve carries signals from the balance organs to the brain

Cochlea

Cochlear nerve carries signals from the cochlea to the brain

Vestibule contains the utricle and saccule balance organs

Eardrum divides the outer ear from the middle ear

Oval window

Ossicles (ear bones) link the eardrum to the oval window

Eustachian tube

Inside the organ of Corti

When sound vibrations pass through the cochlea's fluid, hair cells (red) move up and down. This squashes them, causing hair cells to send signals to the brain. They do the same in the balance organs.

Balancing act

The inner ear houses the fluid-filled organs that help the body keep balance. The three semicircular canals detect rotation of the head in any direction. The utricle and saccule detect when the head – and body – accelerates. These balance organs constantly update the brain, so that it can keep the body upright.

Smell and taste

The senses of smell and taste are closely linked – both detect chemicals. Taste receptors on the tongue detect substances in drink and food. Olfactory (smell) receptors in the nasal cavity pick up odour molecules in air. The two senses enable us to detect all kinds of scents and flavours, good and bad.

Bad air
For centuries, physicians thought diseases were carried by foul-smelling air. This 14th-century physician holds aromatic herbs to his nose to avoid catching his patient's illness.

Left cerebral hemisphere of the brain

Skull bone

Olfactory bulb carries the smell signals to the front of the brain

Branching olfactory nerves connect to the olfactory bulb

Nasal conchae (shelves of bone covered in nasal lining) keep the air inside the nose moist

Nasal cavity connects the nostrils to the throat

Mouth cavity

Tongue surface is covered with papillae, bearing taste buds

Chorda tympani branch of the facial nerve carries taste signals from the front two-thirds of the tongue

One of the muscles that move the tongue

Neuron (nerve cell) carries signals to the brain

Olfactory bulb

Axon of olfactory nerve passes through a channel in the skull bone

Smell receptor cell

Cilia of receptor cell

Odour molecules

Cross-section inside the nose
The nasal cavity's lining (pink) contains thousands of smell receptor cells The cells' hair-like cilia project into the watery mucus of the nasal lining. They detect odour molecules in the air and relay signals to the olfactory nerve, the olfactory bulb, and the brain.

Odour detectors
Odour molecules dissolve in mucus and bind to these cilia, triggering the receptor cells to send signals to the brain. Olfactory receptors can distinguish between 10,000 smells.

Smell and taste pathways
A cross-section through the head shows the routes taken by nerve signals from smell receptors in the nose, and from taste buds in the tongue. In the nasal cavity, branches of the olfactory nerve send signals to the olfactory bulb, which carries the signals to the areas at the front of the brain that identify smells. Taste signals from the front and back of the tongue travel along separate nerves to the brain stem's medulla oblongata. From here they are sent to the area of the brain where tastes are recognized.

Vallate papillae detect bitter tastes

Filiform papillae detect temperature and texture

Vagus nerve carries signals from taste buds in the throat

Nerve carries taste signals from the back of the tongue

Lingual nerve carries touch signals from the front of the tongue

Facial nerve carries taste signals from the front of the tongue

Fungiform papillae detect four different tastes

Taste organ

The muscular tongue mixes and tastes food during chewing. It is covered with pimple-like papillae of different types. These make the tongue sensitive to taste and also to touch and temperature.

Gustatory (taste) area on the left side of the brain

Pons (part of the brain stem) carries signals from the medulla oblongata to the brain

Medulla oblongata (part of the brain stem) receives signals from the facial and glossopharyngeal nerves

Spinal cord

Glossopharyngeal nerve carries taste signals from the rear one-third of the tongue

Throat

Taste receptor cell

Taste pore

Taste hair

Supporting cell

Nerve fibre carries taste signals to the brain

Tongue skin cell

Taste buds

There are around 10,000 taste buds on the tongue, located on certain papillae. Taste molecules dissolve in saliva during chewing and pass into a taste bud through a pore. Here the hairs at the top of the taste receptor cells detect one of five tastes – sweet, sour, salty, bitter, or umami (savoury).

Papillae and taste buds

This SEM shows two types of papillae at the tip of the tongue. The larger, mushroom-shaped fungiform papillae contain taste buds. Spiky filiform papillae give the tongue its rough surface for gripping food during chewing, and their receptors detect the texture and temperature of food.

Hormones

A second control system works alongside the brain and nerve network. The endocrine system is a collection of glands that release chemical messengers, or hormones, into the bloodstream. They control body processes, such as growth and reproduction, by targeting specific body cells and altering their chemical activities. Located in the brain, the hypothalamus links the two control systems.

Hypothalamus

Nerve cells in the front of the hypothalamus produce the hormones oxytocin and ADH

Pituitary stalk connects the hypothalamus to the pituitary gland

Blood vessels carry regulating hormones from the hypothalamus to the front of the pituitary gland

Pituitary gland
Thyroid gland
Thymus gland
Adrenal glands on top of the kidneys
Pancreas
Ovary in female
Testis in male

Endocrine system
The glands that make up the endocrine system lie inside the head and torso. Some endocrine glands, such as the thyroid, are organs in their own right. Other glands are embedded in an organ that also has other functions.

Front lobe of the pituitary gland is stimulated to release its hormones by regulating hormones from the hypothalamus

Thyroid gland
This gland makes two main hormones. Thyroxine targets most body cells and increases their metabolism (chemical processes) to stimulate growth and development. Calcitonin triggers the bones' uptake of calcium from blood.

Right kidney   *Adrenal gland*

Adrenal glands
The two adrenal glands on the kidneys produce corticosteroids, hormones that regulate the levels of salt and water in the blood, speed up the body's metabolism, and deal with stress. The medulla inside each kidney releases adrenaline, the hormone that prepares the body to deal with threats (see left).

Fight or flight
The hormone adrenaline prepares the body to fight or flee in the face of danger. It does this by rapidly boosting heart and breathing rates and diverting blood and extra glucose (sugar) to the muscles.

Vein carries hormones to the body

Hypothalamus

The almond-sized hypothalamus at the base of the brain controls a range of body activities, sometimes through the pituitary gland. Nerve cells in the rear of the hypothalamus produce regulating hormones that travel in the bloodstream to the front lobe of the pituitary, to stimulate the release of pituitary hormones. Nerve cells in the front of the hypothalamus make two more hormones that nerve fibres carry to the rear of the pituitary.

Nerve cells in the rear of the hypothalamus release regulating hormones into the blood vessels supplying the front lobe

Pancreas

The pancreas has two roles. Most of its tissues are gland cells that make digestive enzymes for release along ducts into the small intestine. The endocrine tissues release the hormones insulin and glucagon directly into the bloodstream. These two hormones maintain steady levels of glucose – the sugar removed from food to fuel the body – in the blood.

Nerve fibres carry oxytocin and ADH to the rear lobe of the pituitary gland

Artery (cut) carries fresh blood to the pituitary

Pancreatic islets

The tissue inside the pancreas is dotted with more than one million clusters of cells called islets of Langerhans (centre). In the 1890s, scientists discovered the cells released secretions, later called hormones.

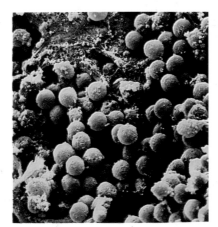

Sir Frederick Banting (1891–1941)

Charles Best (1899–1978)

The insulin story

A lack of the hormone insulin in the body causes a serious condition called diabetes, where blood glucose levels soar. In 1922, Canadian Frederick Banting and American Charles Best successfully extracted insulin so that it could be used to treat and control this disorder.

Rear lobe of the pituitary gland stores and releases ADH and oxytocin

Pituitary gland

The pea-sized pituitary gland is attached to the base of the brain and has separate front and rear parts, or lobes. Front lobe cells make six hormones that affect metabolism, growth, and reproduction, usually by triggering another gland to release hormones. The rear lobe stores and releases anti-diuretic hormone (ADH), which controls urine's water levels, and oxytocin, which makes the uterus contract during labour.

Thymus gland

The thymus gland is large in childhood but shrinks in adult life. During a child's early years, it produces two hormones that ensure the normal development of white blood cells called T cells, or T lymphocytes. These identify and destroy disease-causing organisms, such as bacteria. This SEM shows undeveloped T cells (yellow) in the thymus gland.

The heart

Organ storage
In Egyptians mummies, most body organs were removed and stored in jars such as these. The heart was left in place, ready for the afterlife.

The ancient Egyptians believed the heart housed the soul. For the Greeks it was the seat of love and intelligence. In fact it is an extraordinarily reliable, muscular pump, with a separate right and left side. Each side has two linked chambers – an upper, thin-walled atrium and a larger, thick-walled ventricle below. The right ventricle pumps oxygen-poor blood to the lungs to pick up oxygen and then back to the left atrium. The left ventricle pumps oxygen-rich blood around the body and back to the right atrium. To do this, the heart beats some billion times in an average lifetime.

The right connections
Italian anatomist Andrea Cesalp (1519–1603) realized how the he connects to the main blood vess and the lungs, but not how the circulatory system works (p. 44)

Right coronary artery

Aorta

Left coronary artery

Coronary vein

Coronary sinus (main coronary vein)

Small connecting blood vessels

Main branch of the left coronary artery

Valve open

Valve close

Blood flows away from the heart

Blood pushes through the open valve as the heart contracts

Blood flows back and shuts the valve as the heart relaxes

Blood is pumped out of the heart

Valves at work
Valves ensure the one-way flow of blood. The aortic and pulmonary valves at the two exits from the hea have pocket-shaped flaps of tissue. When the heart contracts, blood pushes its way out, pressing the fla open. When the heart relaxes, blood tries to flow back, pressing the flaps shut.

Coronary circulation
The heart's muscular wall has its own blood supply called the coronary circulation, which delivers oxygen to keep the heart beating. Left and right coronary arteries stem from the aorta and branch out to carry oxygen-rich blood to all parts of the heart wall. Oxygen-poor blood is taken by coronary veins to the coronary sinus. This large vein at the back of the heart empties blood into the right atrium, ready to go round the heart again.

Heart rate
The average adult heart beats 60–80 times, pumping up to 6 litres (11 pints) of blood, every minute. Each beat creates a pressure surge through the body's arteries. This pulse can be felt in the artery in the wrist. During activity, the muscles need more oxygen and nutrients, so the heart beats faster and harder – up to 150 times a minute in the fittest individuals.

achiocephalic artery to
e right side of the head
nd brain, and right arm

perior vena
ava brings
xygen-poor
blood from
e head and
upper body

Right
atrium

ht pulmonary
s bring
gen-rich
od from
right lung

Tricuspid
valve

Right
ventricle

Right ventricle
wall is thinner
than the left

ferior vena cava
gs oxygen-poor
blood from the
domen and legs

escending aorta
kes oxygen-rich
ood to the lower
body and legs

Left common
carotid artery
to the left side
of the head
and brain

Left subclavian
artery to the
left arm

Aorta

Pulmonary artery
takes oxygen-
poor blood to
the lungs

Left atrium

Left pulmonary veins
bring oxygen-rich blood
from the left lung

Pulmonary
valve

Aortic
valve

Bicuspid
valve

Thick
muscular
wall of left
ventricle

Left
ventricle

Septum separates the left
and right sides of the heart

Inside the heart

This cutaway reveals the atria and ventricles.
The muscular ventricle walls contract to pump
blood out of the heart. The wall of the left ventricle,
which pumps blood to the whole body, is thicker
than that of the right, which pumps blood a shorter
distance to the lungs. In just one day, the ventricles
pump up to 15,000 litres (3,300 gallons) of blood.

How the heart beats

Natural pacemaker cells in
the right atrium wall produce
electrical signals to maintain
a regular heartbeat. With
each beat, the left side of the
heart takes in oxygen-rich
blood from the lungs and
pumps it around the body,
while the right side receives
oxygen-poor blood from the
body and pumps it to the
lungs to pick up oxygen.

Blood enters
from the body

Blood
enters
from
the
lungs

Muscular
walls
relax

1 Relax and refill

When the cardiac muscle
relaxes, blood flows in under low
pressure to the right atrium from
the body, and to the left atrium
from the lungs.

Atrial
walls
contract

Tricuspid
valve opens

Bicuspid
valve
opens

2 Atria contract

An electrical signal from the
pacemaker cells causes the atria to
contract. This pumps blood into the
ventricles, through their tricuspid
and bicuspid valves.

Blood out to
the body

Blood
out to
the
lungs

Pulmonary
valve opens

Aortic
valve
opens

Tricuspid
valve closes

Ventricle
walls contract

Bicuspid
valve
closes

3 Ventricles contract

The electrical signal passes
through the ventricle walls, so they
contract. Blood is forced into the
aorta and pulmonary artery, and
the ventricles valves snap shut –
producing the heartbeat you hear.

In circulation

The body's trillions of cells need a constant supply of oxygen, nutrients, and other essentials, and the constant removal of wastes. The heart pumps blood around the body, delivering essentials to cells through a vast network of blood vessels. A second transport system, called the lymphatic system, drains excess fluid from the tissues. The two systems also play key parts in fighting disease.

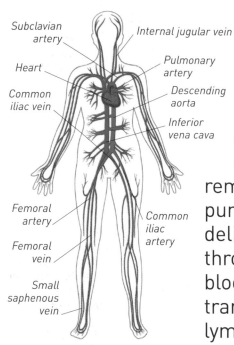

Subclavian artery
Internal jugular vein
Heart
Pulmonary artery
Common iliac vein
Descending aorta
Inferior vena cava
Femoral artery
Common iliac artery
Femoral vein
Small saphenous vein

Circulatory system

Arteries carry oxygen-rich blood from the heart to body tissues, and veins return oxygen-poor blood from the tissues to the heart. Capillaries, too small to be seen here, carry blood through the tissues and connect arteries to veins.

William Harvey, with King Charles I (seated)

Round and round

Until the 17th century, blood was thought to flow backwards and forwards inside arteries and veins. Experiments by English physician William Harvey (1578–1657) showed how the heart pumped blood around the body in one direction.

Blood vessels of the leg

The external iliac artery carries oxygen-rich blood from the heart to the leg. Here it divides into branches that then subdivide to form the microscopic capillaries that deliver oxygen and nutrients to cells, and remove their waste products. The capillaries then rejoin, forming larger vessels that connect into the network of major veins that carry oxygen-poor blood from the leg back towards the heart.

Small saphenous vein carries blood from the foot and lower leg

Small posterior tibial arteries supply blood to the foot and lower leg

Vein valves

Harvey based his theory of blood circulation on careful study, not tradition. His approach marked the beginning of scientific medicine. Harvey's illustrations show how the blood in veins always flows towards the heart. Valves, here marked by letters, prevent it from seeping backwards.

External iliac artery
Extern iliac ve
Pelvis (hip bo
Femoral carries blood fro the thigh
Branc of fem artery suppli blood the th
Great saphenous vein carries blood from foot and le

Ves investiga

Swiss-born anato Albrecht von H (1708–77) investig how muscle in the of smaller arte could contract or r to vary the amou blood flowing particular body

...ood vessels

h every heartbeat, an artery's
ls expand and shrink as blood
m the heart surges through it
igh pressure. Veins carry blood
rning from capillaries at low
ssure, so their wall layers are
nner and less muscular. Just
cell thick, capillary walls let
d and oxygen pass from blood
the surrounding tissues.

Artery

- Outer covering of connective tissue
- Thick muscle layer
- Layer of elastic tissue
- Inner lining

Vein

- Thin muscle layer
- Valve stops blood flowing backwards

Capillary

- Wall made of a single layer of cells
- Cell nucleus

...ighting infection

ry day, the body is exposed to pathogens –
croscopic organisms, such as bacteria and viruses,
t cause disease if they invade the body's tissues
d bloodstream. White blood cells in the
culatory and lymphatic systems form the
dy's immune, or defence, system. Some
rol the body and search for invaders to
stroy. Others attack specific pathogens
d retain a memory of them, in case the
ne pathogens return to infect the body.

- Thymus gland ocesses hocytes
- Lymph vessels drain lymph from the tissues
- Lymph empties into the blood at the subclavian artery
- acic
- Spleen produces large numbers of lymphocytes
- mph odes ered und roin

...mphatic system

network of vessels drains
ss fluid from the body's
es and returns it to the
dstream. The lymphatic
m has no pump, instead the
ractions of skeletal muscles
the fluid, called lymph, along
mph vessels. As it flows,
h passes through small
lings called lymph nodes.

Immune system

The macrophages and lymphocytes –
white blood cells also called T and B
cells – of the immune system respond
to the invasion of pathogens by
detecting and destroying them.

Macrophage

Shigella bacterium

1 Capturing a pathogen

Macrophages are white blood
cells that hunt for pathogens in
the body's tissues. This one has
captured a bacterium called
Shigella and will eat it up.

Antigens (remains of the destroyed bacterium)

2 Recognizing antigens

The macrophage
displays antigens,
or the remains of
the bacterium,
on its surface, to
activate a helper
T cell.

Antibodies attach themselves to a Shigella bacterium

5 Disabling the pathogen

Antibodies bind to the antigens
on the *Shigella* bacterium's surface.
This tags it for macrophages or other
white blood cells to destroy.

Antibody

Helper T cell

B cell

4 Making antibodies

Plasma cells
release billions of
antibody molecules
into the blood and
lymph. The antibodies
track down any *Shigella*
bacteria present in the body.

3 Spurred into action

The helper T cell releases
substances that switch on a B cell
that targets *Shigella*. The B cell
multiplies to produce plasma cells.

Plasma cell

The blood

Feeding on blood
Leeches and vampire bats feed on the blood of other animals. This scene from the 1978 film *Nosferatu* shows a mythical human vampire feeding on blood to gain immortality.

Red blood cell has no nucleus and a dimpled shape

An average adult has 5 litres (9 pints) of blood coursing around the body. Each drop of blood consists of millions of cells floating in liquid plasma. Red blood cells deliver essential oxygen to the body's tissues, while defence cells fight off infections. Blood also distributes heat to keep the body at a steady 37°C (98.6°F) – the ideal temperature for cells to function.

Blood transfusions
Before the discovery of blood groups, the transfusion (transfer) of blood from a donor – usually a healthy person, but here a dog – to a sick patient, often failed, killing the patient.

Red and white blood cells
Each type of blood cell has a vital role to play in the body. Red blood cells, by far the most numerous, transport oxygen to body cells. White blood cells, including neutrophils and lymphocytes help to defend the body against pathogens, or disease-causing germs. Neutrophils track down pathogens such as disease-causing bacteria, and then eat them. Lymphocytes are part of the immune system that targets and destroys specific germs. Platelets help to seal wounds by forming blood clots.

Heart pumps blood around the body

Lungs transfer oxygen and carbon dioxide to and from the blood

Liver controls the concentration of many chemicals in the blood

Spleen removes old, worn-out red blood cells, and helps to recycle their iron

Intestines transfer digested nutrients from food into the blood

Three main roles
Blood transports a range of substances, including oxygen, nutrients, and waste products from cells. It also protects the body by carrying white blood cells and forming blood clots. And it controls body temperature by distributing heat produced by organs around the body.

Neutrophil has a nucleus consisting of many lobes

Plasma makes up 55% of blood

White blood cells and platelets make up 1% of blood

Red blood cells make up 44% of blood

Settled blood

Oxygen-rich blood

Oxygen-poor blood

Blood components

If allowed to settle, blood separates into three parts. The red and white blood cells float in a yellow liquid called plasma. This is mainly water containing over 100 substances including oxygen, nutrients, blood proteins, hormones, and wastes.

Changing colour

Blood takes its colour from the red blood cells. When they pick up oxygen in the lungs, blood turns bright red. Once they unload oxygen in the tissues, blood turns a darker shade of red.

Blood groups

Austrian-American scientist Karl Landsteiner (1868–1943) found that people belonged to one of four blood groups: A, B, AB, or O. Doctors can now match up blood types to avoid a body rejecting a blood transfusion from the wrong blood group.

Oxygen carrier

The protein haemoglobin carries oxygen and gives red blood cells their colour. This computer-generated image shows the structure of its molecules. Each molecule contains four iron atoms (yellow). The iron atoms bind oxygen in the lungs, where oxygen is abundant, and release it wherever oxygen is in short supply in the body.

Lymphocyte has a nucleus that fills most of the cell

Platelet is a cell fragment rather than a cell

Forming blood clots

This cross-section of a skin wound shows how blood reacts. Platelets stick together to briefly form a plug. They also release chemicals that convert a blood protein into threads of fibrin, which trap blood cells to form a jelly-like clot. White blood cells destroy any invading bacteria. The clot dries out to form a protective scab over the tissues while they repair themselves.

A net of fibrin threads traps the blood cells

Scab eventually forms over wound

Invading germ such as bacteria

White blood cell destroys the germs inside the wound

Epidermis of the skin

Dermis

Platelet

Red blood cell

White blood cell moving to the wound

Blood vessel

Breathing to live

The body can survive without food or water for some time, but soon dies if breathing stops. Breathing brings fresh air containing oxygen into the lungs, and then expels stale air containing waste carbon dioxide.

Nasal cavity (space) connects the nostrils to the throat

Three conchae (shelves of bone covered in nasal lining) keep the air inside the nose moist

Nostril contains nose hairs to filter out dirt

Mouth cavity

Oesophagus

Tongue

Epiglottis

Vocal cords

Larynx (voice box)

Trachea (windpipe)

Nasal cavity

Interco
muscle
betwee
the rib

Trachea (windpipe)

R

Right lung

Respiratory system

The respiratory system carries air from outside the body in through its airways – the nasal cavity, throat, larynx, trachea, and its branches – to a pair of lungs. The lungs are protected by the ribs, which also play a part in breathing.

Controlled breathi

Musicians like Charlie Pa (left) and Miles Davis need g breath control to play the saxoph trumpet, and other wind instrume Precisely timed contractions o diaphragm and rib muscles push bu of air out of the mouth and into instrument. Blowing with varying f and duration produces different n

Upper airways

The lungs' delicate tissues are easily damaged by dir particles, which must be removed in the upper airwa after inhalation (breathing in). Nostril hairs filter out larger dirt particles. Sticky mucus covering th nasal lining traps dust and bacteria. T filtered air then passes into th larynx and on to the lu

Larynx

During breathing, air passes from the throat, through the larynx, to the trachea (windpipe). The larynx, also called the voice box, is made of nine pieces of cartilage. During swallowing, the entrance to the larynx is covered by a flap of cartilage called the epiglottis, to prevent food from entering the trachea. The vocal cords are two membrane-covered ligaments that produce sound (see below).

Epiglottis covers [ent]rance to the larynx [during] swallowing

[F]at

[Ad]am's [appl]e" at [the] front [of the] [th]yroid [car]tilage

[Vo]cal cord

Cartilage ring in trachea

Trachea (windpipe)

Cross-section of the larynx from the side

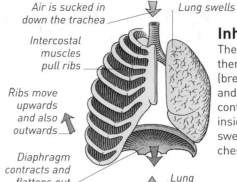

Air is sucked in down the trachea

Lung swells

Intercostal muscles pull ribs

Ribs move upwards and also outwards

Diaphragm contracts and flattens out

Inhalation

The lungs cannot move by themselves. For inhalation (breathing in), the diaphragm and intercostal muscles contract to expand the space inside the chest. As the lungs swell to fill the expanded chest, air is sucked in.

Lung shrinks

Air is blown out

Ribs move inwards and downwards

Diaphragm relaxes back into a dome shape

Exhalation

For exhalation (breathing out), the diaphragm and intercostal muscles relax. The rib cage falls and the diaphragm is pushed up by the organs below it. This squeezes the lungs, and air is forced back outside.

Closed   **Open**

[Vo]cal cords

[Insi]de the throat, when the vocal cords are [rela]xed, they open to let air in and out for [brea]thing. To make sounds, they are pulled [tight] as controlled bursts of air are pushed [out,] making the closed vocal cords vibrate. [The] tongue and lips turn sounds into speech.

Ribs form a protective cage around the lungs

Intercostal muscle runs between two ribs

[Bre]athing and burning

[Engli]sh physician John Mayow [(164)1–79) showed that if a burning [cand]le and a small animal were put in a [seale]d jar, the candle went out and the [anim]al died, as part of the air was used [up. H]e realized the same part of air [(later] named oxygen) was used in the [proce]sses of breathing and burning.

Trachea (windpipe)

Heart

Left lung

Two pleural membranes (shown cut away) lubricate each lung to allow smooth movements

Right lung

Diaphragm is a dome-shaped muscle that squeezes the lungs when we breath out

Inside the chest

The ribs and the intercostal muscles are shown cut away to reveal the lungs and diaphragm. When resting, the body breathes at a rate of around 15 times a minute. During exercise, the need for oxygen increases, and so the rate rises up to 50 times a minute.

Inside the lungs

The lungs are filled with millions of microscopic air sacs called alveoli, each wrapped in a mesh of tiny blood vessels. Alveoli take oxygen from the air we breathe in and pass it into the bloodstream, which delivers oxygen to every body cell to release energy from food in a chemical process known as cell respiration. In exchange, the waste product, carbon dioxide, travels in the bloodstream to the alveoli, where it is expelled.

All-over respiration
Italian scientist Lazzaro Spallanzani (1729–99) proposed that respiration took place not just in the lungs, but in every cell of the body. He also discovered that blood delivered oxygen to body tissues and carried away carbon dioxide.

Upper lobe of the right lung

Branch of the right bronchus

Pulmonary artery is coloured blue to show it carries oxygen-poor blood

Pulmonary vein is coloured red to show it carries oxygen-rich blood

Small bronchus

Terminal (end) bronchioles are the narrowest bronchioles

Middle lobe of the right lung

Bottom lobe of the right lung

Oxygen gets its name
French chemist Antoine Lavoisier (1743–94) showed that a candle burned using part of the air (a gas he called oxygen) and produced a waste gas (now called carbon dioxide). He suggested animals live by burning food inside the lungs using the oxygen in air – a process he called respiration.

X-ray of the bronchial tree
A branching system of tubes carries air all through the lungs. The trachea divides into two bronchi, one to each lung. Each bronchus splits into many smaller bronchi, then bronchioles, and finally terminal bronchioles, narrower than a hair.

Micro-bubbles
This SEM shows red blood cells in a tiny artery in lung tissue. Surrounding the blood vessel are air-filled, bubble-like alveoli, each measuring less than 0.1 mm (0.004 in) across.

Where gas exchange happens
The lungs' 300 million alveoli provide a combined surface area for gas exchange the size of a tennis-court. Around each alveolus is a network of blood capillaries that exchange gases with the alveolus.

Terminal bronchiole

Branch of the pulmonary artery

Branch of the pulmonary vein

Alveoli

Capillary network around the alveolus

Trachea (windpipe)

Aorta carries oxygen-rich blood from the heart

Pulmonary artery carries oxygen-poor blood to the lungs

Upper lobe of the left lung

Oxygen-poor blood rich in carbon dioxide

Carbon dioxide passes into the alveolus from the blood

Stale air leaves the alveolus by the terminal bronchiole

Gas exchange
The walls of an alveolus and the capillary around it are just 0.001 mm (0.00004 in) thick. Oxygen from the alveolus passes into the blood. Carbon dioxide moves in the opposite direction.

Oxygen passes from air in the alveolus into the blood

Blood rich in picked-up oxygen

Capillary

Fresh air enters the alveolus from the terminal bronchiole

Lungs and heart
The right lung (here cut away to reveal its airways) has three lobes. The left lung has two, and leaves space for the heart. Oxygen-poor blood flows a short distance from the right side of the heart along the pulmonary arteries to the lungs, where it is recharged with oxygen and discharges carbon dioxide. The oxygen-rich blood travels along the pulmonary veins to the heart's left side and is then pumped around the whole body.

rior vena cava ers oxygen-poor d to the heart

Heart (pp. 42–43)

Descending aorta carries oxygen-rich blood to the lower body

Lower lobe of the left lung

Eating

Eating food is essential for life. Food supplies the nutrients – a mixture of carbohydrates, proteins, fats, and other substances – that give the bod[y] energy and provide the building blocks for growth and repair. To release these nutrients, food must be processed both mechanically and chemically, by chewing, swallowing, and digesting.

Parotid salivary gland

Nasal cavity

Soft palate

Parotid duct

Pharynx (throat)

Tongue

Teeth

Sublingual duct

Sublingual salivary gland

Submandibular duct

Submandibular salivary gland

Epiglottis

Oesophagus

Trachea (windpipe)

Oesoph[agus]

Liver

Stor[...]

Small intestine

Anus

Large intes[...]

Digestive system
A long tube that runs from the mouth to the anus, the digestive system includes the oesophagus (gullet), stomach, and small and large intestines. The liver, too, is linked to digestion.

Inside the mouth
When food enters the mouth, taste bud[s] on the tongue sample it to see how delicious or unpleasant it is. As teeth c[ut] and crush the food, salivary glands squ[eeze] watery saliva along ducts into the mouth, to bind and lubricate th[e] food particles together. Sa[liva] also contains an enz[yme] that starts break[ing] down starch i[n] the food.

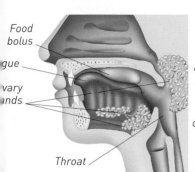

Food bolus
gue
vary
nds

Throat

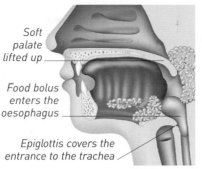

Soft palate lifted up

Food bolus enters the oesophagus

Epiglottis covers the entrance to the trachea

Contracted muscle

Food bolus

Relaxed muscle

ewing a mouthful

we chew, our teeth cut and crush
d into small particles. Our tongue
es the food with the sticky mucus
aliva to form a compact, slippery
us, or ball of food, and pushes it
kwards into the throat.

Swallowing

The tongue pushing back triggers
the muscles in the throat to
contract, moving the bolus into the
oesophagus. The soft palate and
epiglottis stop food entering the
nasal cavity and trachea (windpipe).

Peristalsis

Peristalsis, or waves
of muscle contractions,
squeezes the bolus down
the oesophagus to the
stomach, and also
through the intestines.

A balanced diet

is meal includes the six main
ients we need from our food.
Rice contains carbohydrates
rches and sugars) for energy.
sh and meat contain proteins
build and maintain the body,
plus a little fat, for energy.
egetables (and fruit) are rich
vitamins and minerals that
help cells to work well, and
fibre that helps the intestinal
muscles work better.

Energy release

Running, like any physical
activity, requires the energy that
comes from food. The digestive
process converts food starches
into sugars and fats into fatty
acids. Broken down inside
muscle cells, these fuels
release energy for movement.

eth

teeth break up food to make it easier to swallow and digest.
ing childhood, milk teeth are replaced by a larger set of adult,
ermanent, teeth. These include chisel-like incisors that cut
slice at the front, pointed canines that grip
tear, and flat premolars and molars
crush and grind at the back.

Root anchors
tooth in jaw bone

Adult tooth
will push out
milk tooth as
it grows

Upper third molar
(wisdom tooth) may
or may not appear

Enamel is the tooth's
hard surface material

Dentine supports
the enamel

Pulp is the soft tissue
inside the central cavity

Crown

Gum forms a tight
collar around the
base of the crown

Root

Cement layer
secures the
root of the tooth
in position

Jaw bone

Blood vessels
and nerves
supply the
living pulp
tissue

e-year teeth

irst 20 milk teeth appear from
ge of six months. From about
ars they begin to fall out.

Full set of adult teeth

By early adulthood, all 32 adult teeth have
come through. Each half jaw has two incisors,
one canine, two premolars, and three molars.

Inside a tooth

Bone-like dentine forms the tooth's root and
supports a rock-hard crown of non-living enamel
for grinding up food. The central cavity contains
living pulp tissue fed by blood vessels and by nerve
endings that sense pressure as we bite and chew.

Digestion

After swallowing, it takes about ten seconds for chewed food to reach the stomach, where digestion really gets under way. The stomach starts to break down food with enzymes (chemical digesters) and churns it into liquid chyme, which it releases slowly into the small intestine. Here, further enzymes digest food into its simplest components. These nutrients are then absorbed into the bloodstream and circulated to the body's cells.

Food-processor

The stomach is a J-shaped bag that expands as it receives food through the oesophagus (gullet) and processes it for the next few hours. Its muscular wall contracts to churn up the food, while acidic gastric (stomach) juice digests the food's proteins. The end result is a soupy liquid called chyme. This is released slowly into the small intestine.

The body's chemical factory

Our largest internal organ, the liver helps to balance the chemical make-up of blood. As oxygen-rich blood from the heart and nutrient-rich blood from the intestines pass through the liver, it releases nutrients into the bloodstream for circulation, or stores them for future use. It also makes bile (see below), removes poisons from the blood, destroys bacteria, and recycles worn-out red blood cells. All of this activity generates heat that helps keep the body warm.

Gastric pits

Millions of gastric pits dot the stomach's lining. Through these tiny holes, gastric glands release gastric juice into the stomach. The juice produces an enzyme that digests the proteins in food. Mucus in the juice coats the stomach

The intestines

The small intestine is about 6 m (20 ft) long and has three sections. The short duodenum receives chyme from the stomach and digestive fluids (bile and pancreatic juice) from the liver and pancreas. In the jejunum and ileum, digestion is completed and nutrients are absorbed. The large intestine is just 1.5 m (5 ft) long. Here, watery waste from the ileum dries out as it passes

Oesophagus

Left lobe of the liver

Stomach has a muscular wall

Transverse colon conceals the duodenum connecting the stomach to the jejunum

Jejunum is the middle section of the small intestine

Descending colon

Right lobe of the liver

Gall bladder stores bile

Ascending colon

Sigmoid (S-shaped) colon

Claude Bernard

Rectum stores the faeces before release

Anus opens to release faeces

Ileum is the final and longest section of the small intestine

large intestine

Appendix contains a reservoir of useful gut bacteria

Gall bladder

Folded lining of the gall bladder

Right kidney

Duodenum

Bile duct carries bile from the gall bladder

Opening of the combined pancreatic and bile ducts into the duodenum

Common hepatic duct from liver to gall bladder

Pancreas

Left kidney

Spleen

Main pancreatic duct

Folded lining of the duodenum

Pancreatic tissues contain the enzyme-producing cells

Claude Bernard

French scientist Claude Bernard (1813–78) proved that substances from the pancreas helped break down fat, and that the main processes of digestion occur in the small intestine. He also pioneered the idea of homeostasis, that constant conditions, such as temperature or correct water balance, are maintained inside the body.

Digestive waste disposal

After eating, it takes 20–44 hours for the indigestible waste, in the form of bacteria-laden faeces, to reach the rectum for release.

Pancreatic enzymes

The pancreas releases pancreatic juice into the duodenum. The pancreatic juice contains enzymes that digest the carbohydrates, proteins, and fats in food, which are passed on from the stomach.

Intestinal lining

Enzymes on these villi in the small intestine complete the digestion of food into its simplest components: glucose (sugar), amino acids, and fatty acids. Those nutrients are then absorbed through the villi and carried away by blood capillaries and the lymphatic system.

Gall bladder and bile

The gall bladder is a stretchy bag that stores green-coloured, liquid bile, then releases it into the duodenum when food arrives. Bile is produced in the liver and breaks up fats and oils into tiny droplets so they can be digested more rapidly.

Waste disposal

Body cells continually release waste substances, such as urea made by the liver, into the bloodstream. If left to build up, they would poison the body. The urinary system disposes of waste by cleansing the blood as it passes through a pair of kidneys. It also removes excess water to ensure the body's water content stays the same.

Bladder control

When a baby's bladder is full of urine, the stretch receptors in its muscular wall automatically tell it to empty. Young children learn to control this reflex action.

Giant of ancient Greece

The Greek philosopher Aristotle (384–322 BCE) challenged ideas about anatomy by looking inside real bodies of animals and huma and recording what he saw. He provided the first descriptions of urinary system and how it works

Kidney cortex contains blood capillaries and Bowman's capsules

Nephron (filtering unit) consists of a glomerulus and a looping tubule

Capillary reabsorbs nutrients and water from the tubule

Glomerulus inside a Bowman's capsule filters blood

Bowman's capsule

Medulla contains blood vessels and urine-forming tubules

Tubule

U-shaped loop of Henle

Collecting duct

Filtering unit

Each kidney's blood-filtering unit, or nephron, links to a long tubule. This loops from the cortex to the medulla and back, then joins a collecting duct. As fluid filtered from blood passes along the nephron, useful substances are absorbed back into the bloodstream, leaving waste urine to flow into the collecting duct.

Capsules and loops

English surgeon and scientist Willia Bowman (1816–92) identified the capsule that bears his name. The U-shaped loop of Henle was later described by the German anatomist Jakob Henle (1809–

William Bowman

Bowman's capsule

Each capsule surrounds a glomerulus, or cluster of capillaries. They filter the blood and produce a fluid. It contains not only waste, but also substances such as glucose (sugar), which are useful to the body.

Small artery entering the glomerulus

Small artery leaving glome

Space w filtered collects

Capillary of the glomerulus

Start of tubule

Renal vein carries cleansed blood from the kidney

Renal artery delivers blood to the kidney

Cross-section of left kidney shows the internal structure

Cortex is the outer part of the kidney

Medulla consists of pyramid-shaped segments

Pelvis of the kidney

Protective capsule surrounds kidney

Urinary system

The two kidneys contain two million nephrons that process 1,750 litres (385 gallons) of blood per day, producing about 1.5 litres (2.5 pints) of urine. The urine goes from a kidney's hollow pelvis into a ureter. This long tube's muscular walls squeeze urine down to the bag-like bladder, which stores the urine until a person wants to urinate. A ring of muscle, the sphincter, mostly holds the bladder exit tightly closed. When the sphincter is relaxed, urine leaves the body through a tube called the urethra.

Urinary X-ray

Using a special red dye injected into the bloodstream, this X-ray shows the flow of urine through the body. The dye is filtered out of the blood into urine through the kidney's nephrons. Then it passes into the pelvis at the centre of each kidney, down the ureters, and into the bladder.

Right kidney

Inferior vena cava

Aorta

Left ureter

Right ureter squeezes urine towards bladder

Common iliac artery

Common iliac vein

Female urinary system

Bladder (shown with section removed)

Muscular wall of the bladder

Folds in lining smooth out as bladder fills with urine

Internal sphincter muscle

Urethra carries urine out of the body

Opening of ureter

Male bladder

Right ureter

Left ureter

Muscular wall

Exit to the urethra

Sphincter muscle]

Opening of left ureter

Urethra

Bladder control

The bladder's elastic, muscular wall expands as it fills with urine. Receptors send signals to the brain, triggering the need to urinate. As the sphincter relaxes, the bladder muscles squeeze the urine out through the urethra.

Male and female

Like all life forms, humans reproduce to pass on their genes and continue the cycle of life. Male and female reproductive systems produce different sex cells. Sexual intercourse (sex) between a man and a woman brings her eggs and his sperm together. These sex cells contain half of each partner's DNA (genetic instructions), which combine during fertilization inside the woman's body to create a new life. Her uterus then provides the place where the baby will develop.

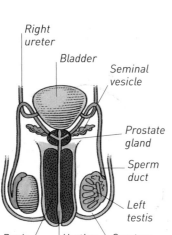

External features

A 1543 guide to anatomy by Vesalius shows the male is more muscular than the female, with wide shoulders, narrow hips, and more facial and body hair. She is more rounded by body fat around the thighs and abdomen, with wide hips and developed breasts.

Right ureter

Bladder

Seminal vesicle

Prostate gland

Sperm duct

Left testis

Penis   *Urethra*   *Scrotum*

Front view of the male reproductive system

Male reproductive organs

This side-view shows one of two testes that hang outside the body in a skin bag called the scrotum. Inside each testis, a hormone stimulates sperm production throughout a man's adult life. During sex, muscle contractions push sperm along two sperm ducts into the urethra and out of the penis.

Bladder

Urethra

Penis

Left testis

Scrotum

Epididymis

Seminal vesicle, together the pros gland, ac fluid to t sperm to nourish stimulate

Prostate gland

The menstrual cycle

Every 28 days, in a woman's menstrual (monthly) cycle, or period, an egg is released from an ovary and the lining of the uterus thickens in order to receive the egg if it is fertilized by a sperm. The cycle is controlled by hormones released by the pituitary gland and by ovaries.

Ovary — Uterus lining breaks down — Vagina — Mature follicle — Fallopian tube — Egg — Egg — Uterus lining

1 First week
The uterus lining, which thickened in the previous period, breaks down and is lost as blood-flow through the vagina.

2 Second week
An egg-containing follicle near the ovary's surface swells as it ripens. The uterus lining begins to grow and thicken again.

3 Third week
Ovulation occurs when the mature follicle releases its egg. The egg is moved along the fallopian tube towards the uterus.

4 Fourth week
The uterus lining is thick and blood-rich. If the egg is fertilized, it sinks into the lining. If not, it is broken down and the cycle begins again.

gnier de Graaf

ch physician and anatomist nier de Graaf (1641–73) did iled research on the male female reproductive ems. In the female system, dentified the ovaries and cribed the tiny bubbles on ovary's surface that appear month. Later scientists zed that each bubble is a follicle with the much ller egg contained within it.

y held osition by a ament

Fallopian tube

Left ovary

Fimbriae

Cervix — Vagina

Front view of the female reproductive system

Female reproductive organs

A woman's ovaries release a gle mature egg each month during her fertile years. It is wafted by fimbriae into the lopian tube that leads to the us. If the egg meets a sperm on after its release, the two and fertilization occurs. This results in a baby that grows inside the greatly expanding us (womb) and is eventually born through the vagina.

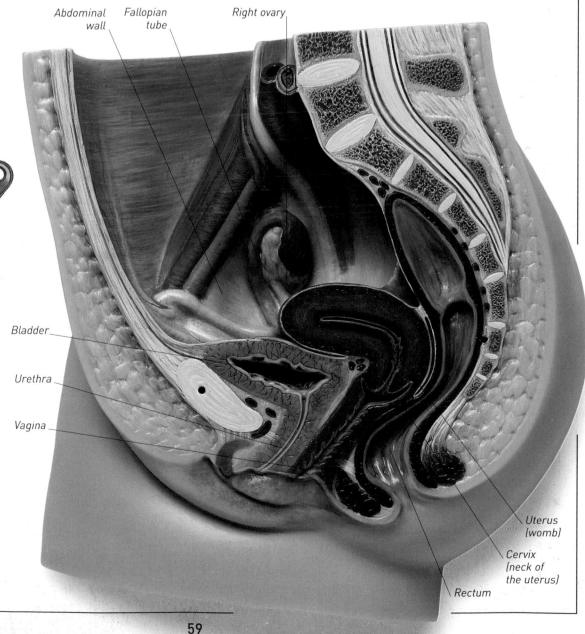

Abdominal wall — Fallopian tube — Right ovary

Bladder

Urethra

Vagina

Uterus (womb)

Cervix (neck of the uterus)

Rectum

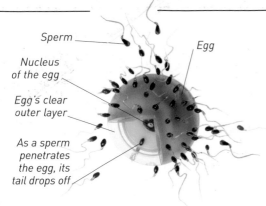

Sperm

Egg

Nucleus of the egg

Egg's clear outer layer

As a sperm penetrates the egg, its tail drops off

Fertilization of an egg

In this cutaway model, one of the sperm trying to get through the outer covering of the egg has succeeded. Its tail has dropped off, and its head (nucleus) will fuse with, or fertilize, the egg's nucleus. No other sperm can now get through.

A new life

Fertilization merges the DNA (genetic instruction carried by a male sperm and female egg. If the fertilized egg, no bigger than the full stop at the end of this sentence, settles in the lining of the woman's uterus, it grows into an embryo and the a fetus. Around 38 weeks after fertilization, the fetus is ready to be born. Muscular contractions the uterus push the baby out through its mother vagina, and the newborn baby takes its first breat

Embryo development

The fertilized egg divides into two cells, then four, eight, and so on. A week after fertilization, it implants in the uterus lining, becoming an embryo. As its cells divide, they form muscle, nerve, and other tissues. By five weeks, the embryo is the size of a pea.

Cluster of 16 cells

Model of a five-week-old embryo

Heart

Arm bud

Developing vertebra of the spine (backbone)

Liver can be seen

Ear beginning to form

Developing eye

Developing mouth

Tail bud

Leg bud

Recognizable limbs

Uterus wall

First embryologist

Italian anatomy professor Hieronymus Fabricius (1537–1619) described the development of unborn babies, or embryos, in humans and in other animals. Known as the founder of embryology, he also named the ovary and predicted its function.

Uterus enlarges to accommodate the growing fetus

All main organs are formed

Umbilical cord

Cervix

Plac

Fetal development

From two months after fertilization through to birth, the baby gradually comes to look human. It is now called a fetus. At two months, it is no bigger than a strawberry but its major organs have formed and its heart is beating. By around nine months, the fetus weighs about 3–4 kg (6.5–9 lb).

1 Two months
The 2.5-cm- (1-in-) long fetus has limbs and its brain is expanding rapidly.

2 Three months
About 8 cm (3 in) long, the fetus looks human and has eyes.

3 Five months
The fetus is 20 cm (8 in long and responds to sound kicking and turning somers

The placenta

The placenta on the wall of the uterus nourishes the fetus. Inside it, blood vessels from the mother and fetus pass close to each other. This allows oxygen and food to pass from the mother's blood into the blood of the fetus, through the umbilical cord. Waste from the fetus flows the other way. After the baby is born, the umbilical cord is clamped and cut. The placenta detaches and comes out.

Fetal blood vessels

Maternal blood vessel

Placenta forms a link between the baby's blood and its mother's blood

Umbilical arteries

...eing the fetus

...asound scans carried ...after about 11 weeks ...ck all is well with the ...s developing inside the ...rus. The scanner beams ...-pitched but harmless ...d waves into the body, ...detects their echoes. ...omputer displays the ...oes as a 3D image.

Blood vessels inside the umbilical cord carry blood to and from the fetus

xpanded uterus ...esses on ...nother's ...dominal organs

Fetus has grown visibly in the past two months

Stretched uterus wall

Cervical plug of thick mucus protects the fetus from infection

Vagina (birth canal)

Cervix will widen for the birth

Amniotic fluid cushions the fetus

Amnion is the membrane containing amniotic fluid in which the baby floats

...s has ...rned ...side ...into ...birth ...sition

Cervix tightly shut

Seven months

Now about 48 cm (19 in) the fetus has finger- and ...ails, and its eyes are open.

5 Nine months

The fetus is fully grown, at about 36 cm (14 in) long. With fully formed lungs, it is ready to be born.

Mother and baby

Many mothers breast-feed their babies. Breast milk gives the baby the nutrients for growth and development in the early months before it can eat solid food. Milk is produced by glands inside the breasts and released when the baby suckles.

Growth and development

From birth to old age, we follow the same pattern of growth and body development. Physical and mental changes turn us from children into adults, and growth stops by our early 20s. The body then matures, and in later years begins to deteriorate. This pattern is controlled, like all of the body's processes, by 23 pairs of chromosomes in the nucleus of every body cell. Each chromosome is made up of deoxyribonucleic acid (DNA). Sections of DNA, called genes, contain the coded instructions that build and maintain the body.

Master molecule
US biologist James Watson (1928–) and British biophysicist Francis Crick (1916–2004) showed that the DNA molecule has two strands that spiral like a twisted ladder. Its rungs hold the code forming the instructions in genes.

Genes and inheritanc
If a man and woman reprodu
they each pass on a set of ge
to their child. The genes that
girl inherited from her moth
and father are mostly identica
but some are different, so her
combination of genes is uniqu

Cell division
Bodies grow by making new cells. Cells reproduce by dividing in two. For most cells, this involves mitosis. Each chromosome duplicates inside a parent cell to produce an identical copy. The copies move apart, and the cell divides to produce two daughter cells that are identical to each other.

Daughter cell grows after division

Nucleus of daughter cell contains 46 chromosomes

Cell's cytoplasm splits to separate daughter cells

Banding pattern on every chromosome is produced by chemicals and used in mapping

Sex chromosome Y is passed on by the father

XY sex chromoson determine that th person is male. A pairing would mal the person female

Pair of matching chromosomes: one is passed on by the mother, the other by the father

Each pair of matching chromosomes may carry different versions of the same gene

Sex chromosor is passed on by father or moth

Position of the gene that, if defective, causes cystic fibrosis

Human genome
Every human cell contains 23 chromosomes, called the genome. Each has a partner. One of each pair is from the mother, one is from the father. Each chromosome has the same genes as its partner, but not always identical versions. It might carry the version of a gene giving blue eyes, but the other chromosome might have the version for brown. While 22 of the chromosome pairs match, the 23rd pair matches only in females and determines a person's sex.

Map of the genome of a man

Chromosome 12 carries over 1,400 genes

2 1 Y X 22
3
4   21
5   20
6   19
7   18
8   17
9   16
10   15
11 12 13 14

owth and the skeleton

ore birth, the skeleton is made of either flexible cartilage or, in skull, membranes reinforced n fibres. As the fetus grows, st of these tissues are fied – replaced by hard e. But the bones of the nium (skull) are incomplete irth, and are connected by anelles, or membranes allow the brain to grow. arly childhood, these too ossified, and the skull es are knitted together. ng childhood, the skull's al bones grow rapidly to h up with the cranium.

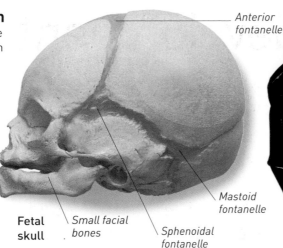

Anterior fontanelle

Mastoid fontanelle

Fetal skull

Small facial bones

Sphenoidal fontanelle

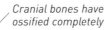

Cranial bones have ossified completely

Facial bones grow rapidly uring childhood

dult tooth shing out milk tooth

r jaw reatly eased n size

Six-year-old skull

Jigsaw-like, fixed suture joint

Puberty and adolescence

During the three to four years of puberty, the body grows rapidly and the reproductive system begins to function. Most girls reach puberty at 10–12 years, and boys at 12–14 years.

A girl's body becomes more rounded, she develops breasts, and her periods start. A boy's body becomes more muscular, his voice deepens, facial hair grows, and he starts producing sperm. Puberty forms part of adolescence, the process that also involves mental changes as teenagers turn into adults.

Later years

In our 50s, ageing becomes noticeable. The skin loses its springiness and develops lines and wrinkles, as in the face of this elderly Native American. The heart and lungs become less efficient, joints stiffen and bones become more fragile, vision is less effective, and brain function decreases. But looking after the body with healthy food and exercise can slow these changes and help us stay healthy well into our 80s.

Chief of the Crow tribe (c. 1906)

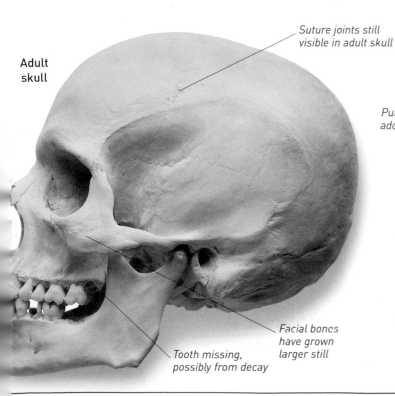

Adult skull

Suture joints still visible in adult skull

Facial bones have grown larger still

Tooth missing, possibly from decay

Young adulthood

Middle age

Old age

Puberty and adolescence

Birth

Death

Life story from cradle to grave

Following birth and childhood, early adulthood is a time of responsibility and becoming a parent. Middle age brings wisdom, and the start of ageing. In old age, the body begins to decline until, eventually, we die. With better food, health care, and sanitation in the developed world, average life expectancy is almost 80 years, twice that of the 16th-century man above.

Future bodies

Advances in biology, medicine, and technology make it possible to repair or improve the human body in new ways, such as bionic limbs and artificial organs. For some people, research using stem cells or hybrid embryos interferes with the sanctity of life. Others predict a world of nanobots, cyborgs, and brain microchips.

Stem cells taken from umbilical cord blood

Stem cells

Doctors believe unspecialized cells, cal[led] stem cells, can be used to repair diseas[ed] or damaged tissues in patients. Stem c[ells] divide to produce a range of cell types a[nd] so can build many types of body tissue.

Gene therapy

Each body cell contains over 20,000 genes, the DNA instructions that build and run it. A faulty gene can cause disease. Scientists hope it will soon be possible to cure some conditions using gene therapy – replacing faulty genes with normal ones carried into body cells by a harmless virus.

Designer children

One day it may be possible to treat a sick child with a faulty gene by using stem cells from a specially designed sibling. First, a number of embryos are created through IVF (in vitro fertilization), where an egg is fertilized outside the body in a laboratory. If it does not have the faulty gene, it is placed in the mother's uterus to develop into a baby. When the designer child is born, stem cells in its discarded umbilical cord are used to treat its sick sibling.

Hybrid embryos

Human embryos are a controversial so[urce] of stem cells. As an alternative, the DN[A] containing nucleus in a cow's egg is replaced by a nucleus from a human s[tem] cell. The cell divides to create a hybrid embryo that is 99.9 per cent human and is a new source of stem cells to research cures for diseases.

Bionic arm is wired to the chest muscles

Sensors monitor signals from the chest muscles and trigger arm and hand movements

Artificial hand and fingers move according to the woman's conscious thoughts

Growing organs
Currently, diseased organs are replaced by transplanting a donor organ from someone else. Using cells from the patient instead, bladder tissue has been grown around a mould (above) and the new bladder was successfully implanted into the patient.

ionic limbs
er this patient lost her arm in an accident, ionic arm was wired to her chest muscles. en she thinks about moving her hand, ssages travel to the muscles, which send out ctrical signals. Sensors pass these to a tiny nputer that tells her arm how to move.

Neuron is one of a network forming a circuit with a microchip

Pillar supports the neuron on the microchip

Brain microchips
This microchip forms a miniature electronic circuit with a network of neurons and can stimulate them to send and receive signals to one another and to the microchip. Future scientists might use neuron–microchip circuits to repair brain damage or boost memory or intelligence.

Medical nanobots
Nanotechnology manipulates atoms and molecules to build tiny machines. These nanobots, or nanorobots, are self-propelled, respond to their surroundings, and can carry out tasks on their own initiative. One day, it may be possible for medical nanobots to detect, diagnose, and repair damage to the body's cells and tissues.

Cyborgs
In the *Terminator* films, actor Arnold Schwarzenegger played the role of a cyborg – a character with increased natural abilities, being part-human, part-machine. Future advances in technology may yet make such hybrids possible.

Eternal life?
Medical advances, such as gene therapy and organ replacement, together with lifestyle changes, could enable everyone to live longer. But what quality of life would there be for a 150-year-old? And how would our crowded planet support so many extra, possibly unproductive, human beings?

Timeline

With each new discovery, scientists have built up a clearer picture of the body and its systems. Even so, there remain many mysteries about the workings of the human body.

c. 160,000 BCE
Modern humans first appear.

c. 2650 BCE
Egyptian Imhotep is the earliest known physician.

c. 1500 BCE
The earliest known medical text, the *Ebers Papyrus*, is written in Egypt.

c. 500 BCE
Greek physician Alcmaeon suggests that brain, and not heart, is the seat of thought and feelings.

c. 420 BCE
Greek physician Hippocrates emphasizes the importance of diagnosis.

c. 280 BCE
Herophilus of Alexandria describes the cerebrum and cerebellum of brain.

Statue of Imhotep c. 2650 BCE

c. 200 CE
Greek-born Roman doctor Claudius Galen describes, incorrectly, how human body works; his teachings are not challenged until the 1500s.

c. 1025
Persian doctor Avicenna publishes the *Canon of Medicine,* which will influence European medicine for the next 500 years.

c. 1280
Syrian doctor Ibn an-Nafis shows that blood circulates around the body.

c. 1316
Italian anatomist Mondino dei Liuzzi publishes his dissection guide *Anatomy*.

c. 1500
Italian artist and scientist Leonardo da Vinci makes anatomical drawings based on his own dissections.

Anatomical drawing by Leonardo da Vinci

1543
Flemish doctor Andreas Vesalius publishes *On the Structure of the Human Body*, which accurately describes human anatomy.

1562
Italian anatomist Bartolomeo Eustachio describes the ear in *The Examination of the Organ of Hearing*.

1590
Dutch spectacle maker, Zacharias Janssen, invents the microscope.

1603
Hieronymus Fabricius, an Italian anatomist, describes the structure of a vein in his book, *On the Valves of Veins.*

1628
English doctor William Harvey describes blood circulation in *On the Movement of the Heart and Blood in Animals.*

1662
French philosopher René Descartes' book, *Treatise of Man*, describes the human body as a machine.

1663
Italian biologist Marcello Malpighi discovers capillaries, the small blood vessels that link arteries and veins.

1664
English doctor Thomas Willis describes the blood supply to the brain.

1665
English physicist Robert Hooke coins the term "cell" for the smallest units of life he sees through his compound microscope.

1672
Dutch anatomist Regnier de Graaf describes the female reproductive system.

Hooke's microscope 1665

1674–77
Antoni van Leeuwenhoek, a Dutch cloth merchant and microscopist, describes human blood cells and sperm cells.

1691
English doctor Clopton Havers describe the microscopic structure of bones.

1775
French chemist Antoine Lavoisier discovers oxygen and later shows that cell respiration consumes oxygen.

1800
French doctor Marie-François Bichat shows that organs are made of groups cells called tissues.

1811
Scottish anatomist Charles Bell shows that nerves are bundles of nerve cells.

1816
French doctor René Laënnec invents the stethoscope to listen to the lungs and heart.

1833
American army surgeon William Beaumont publishes the results of his experiments into the mechanism of digestion.

37
...ech biologist Johannes Purkinje observes ...urons in the brain's cerebellum.

42
...tish surgeon William Bowman describes ...microscopic structure and workings of ...kidney.

An early ophthalmoscope

48
...nch ...entist ...ude Bernard ...scribes the ...rkings of the liver.

51
...man physicist ...rmann von ...mholtz invents the ...thalmoscope, an ...trument for looking ...de the eye.

61
...nch doctor Paul Pierre Broca identifies ...area on the brain that controls speech.

71
...man scientist Wilhelm Kühne coins the ...n "enzyme" for substances that speed up ...mical reactions inside living things.

95
...man physicist Wilhelm Roentgen ...overs X-rays.

01
...l Landsteiner, an Austrian-American ...tor, identifies blood groups, paving the ...for more successful blood transfusions.

05
...ish scientist Ernest Starling coins the ...n "hormone".

30
...erican physiologist Walter Cannon coins ...term "homeostasis" for mechanisms that ...ntain a stable state inside the body.

33
...man electrical engineer Ernst Ruska ...nts the electron microscope.

52
...urgeon Joseph E Murray performs the ...kidney transplant, on identical twins.

52
...e US, Paul Zoll invents the pacemaker ...ntrol an irregular heartbeat.

...unded US soldier ...ives a blood ...sfusion ...g ...d War II

1953
US biologist James Watson and British physicist Francis Crick discover the double-helix structure of DNA.

1958
British doctor Ian Donald uses ultrasound scanning to check the health of a fetus.

1961
US scientist Marshall Nirenberg cracks the genetic code of DNA.

1967
Magnetic resonance imaging (MRI) is first used to see soft tissues inside the body.

1972
Computed tomography (CT) scanning first produces images of human organs.

1980
Doctors perform "keyhole" surgery inside the body through small incisions with the assistance of an endoscope.

1980s
Positron emission tomography (PET) scans first produce images of brain activity.

1982
The first artificial heart, invented by US scientist Robert Jarvik, is transplanted into a patient.

1984
French scientist Luc Montagnier discovers the human immunodeficiency virus (HIV) that results in AIDS.

Blood bag

2001
Scientists perform the first germline gene transfer in animals, to prevent faulty genes being passed on to offspring.

2002
Gene therapy is used to treat an inherited immuno-deficiency disease that leaves the body unable to fight against infection.

Computer display of DNA sequencing

2003
Scientists publish results of the Human Genome Project, identifying the DNA sequence of a full set of chromosomes.

2006
A urinary bladder, grown in the laboratory from a patient's own cells, is successfully transplanted to replace a damaged organ.

2007
Thought to be useless, the appendix is shown to hold a back-up reservoir of bacteria that is essential to the workings of the large intestine.

2008
Dutch geneticist Marjolein Kreik becomes the first woman to have her genome sequenced.

2010
DaVinci, a surgical robot, performs the world's first all-robotic surgery in Montreal, Canada.

Surgical robot, DaVinci

2013
Scientists in Japan create a functional human liver from skin and blood stem cells.

Find out more

Listen out for news stories about the latest discoveries in medical science, and documentaries about the human body and how it works. Look out for special exhibitions at museums near you, or search in your local library and online. You also have your own body to study! Take good care of it by eating healthily and exercising regularly.

The old operating theat
This 19th-century operating theatre at t
old site of St Thomas' hospital in Lond
predates anaesthetics. Surgeons wor
quickly to minimize a patient's suffer
during amputations and other operatic
Medical students watched from tie
stands around the operating ta

Anatomy on show
Body Worlds is a touring display of "plastinates" – real human bodies that are cleverly preserved in exciting poses to reveal inner organs and tissues. Since 1995, more than 20 million people have seen the exhibition worldwide.

Skin is removed to reveal the muscles, major organs, and blood vessels

One of the plastinates at the *Body Worlds* exhibition

PLACES TO VISIT

CITÉ DES SCIENCES, PARIS, FRANCE
- Interactive displays of the human body
- Detailed explorations of DNA discoveries

FRANKLIN INSTITUTE, PHILADELPHIA, USA
- Giant walk-through heart
- *Melting humans* exhibit showing internal organs and systems

HALL OF SCIENCE, NEW YORK, USA
- Infrared camera maps your body's hot spots
- Lots of hands-on exhibits to explore perceptions, molecules, and health

THE HUNTERIAN, GLASGOW, UK
- Life-size plaster casts of dissections
- Anatomical specimens preserved in jars
- Scientific instruments

SCIENCE MUSEUM, LONDON, UK
- *Who am I?* gallery on genetics and identity
- Exhibits on the history of medicine

DUNDEE SCIENCE CENTRE, DUNDEE, UK
- Lots on the senses
- Interactive keyhole surgery exhibit
- Face-morphing

THACKRAY MUSEUM, UK
- Exhibits on surgery and Sherlock Bones

LA SPECOLA, FLORENCE, ITALY
- Anatomical wax models of 18th-century dissected bodies

Early stethoscope at the
Science Museum, London

alk-in body

he Health Museum in Houston,
as, USA, visitors can take a larger-
n-life tour through the human body –
uding this arch created by a giant
kbone and ribs. The Amazing Body
ilion features exciting interactive
eriences including a giant eyeball
a walk-through brain, and hands-
xhibits about health and well-being.

Giant body sculpture

Australian artist Ron Mueck's *Mask II* is a giant self-portrait of the artist sleeping and is sculpted from resin and fibre glass. Visits to art galleries to see sculptures and paintings can reveal much about the variety of the human form.

*Acrobat's brain
ontrols balance,
ure, and precise
movements*

ROBATICS

hing ballet and circus shows like
Cirque du Soleil provides a great
ortunity to marvel at the strength,
bility, and grace of the human body.

*Muscle and
joint flexibility
is achieved
by constant
training*

USEFUL WEBSITES

- A great website from the BBC covering all aspects of the body:
  www.bbc.co.uk/science/humanbody
- A fun, animated guide to the human body:
  www.brainpop.com/health
- A comprehensive guide to blood, from platelets to plasma – this website has several other body topics, too:
  health.howstuffworks.com/blood
- A website for young people, with tips on keeping healthy:
  kidshealth.org/kids

Glossary

Blood vessels supplying the lower arm and hand

ABDOMEN The lower part of the torso between the chest and hips.

ADOLESCENCE The period of physical and mental changes that occur during the teenage years and mark the transition from childhood to adulthood.

ALVEOLI The microscopic air bags in the lungs through which oxygen enters the blood and carbon dioxide leaves it.

AMNIOTIC FLUID A liquid that surrounds the fetus inside its mother's uterus. It protects the fetus from knocks and jolts.

ANATOMY The study of the structure of the human body.

ANTIBODY A substance released by cells called lymphocytes, which marks an invading pathogen or germ for destruction.

ARTERY A blood vessel that carries blood from the heart towards the body tissues.

ATOM The smallest particle of an element, such as carbon or hydrogen, that can exist.

BACTERIA A type of microorganism. Some bacteria are pathogens (germs) that cause disease in humans.

BILE A fluid delivered from the liver to the intestine to aid digestion.

Acupuncture needles inserted into the skin to provide pain relief

BLOOD VESSEL A tube, such as an artery, vein, or capillary, that transports blood around the body.

CAPILLARY A microscopic blood vessel that links arteries to veins.

CARTILAGE A tough, flexible tissue that supports the nose, ears, and other body parts, and covers bones' ends in joints.

CELL One of the trillions of microscopic living units that make up a human body.

CHROMOSOME One of 46 packages of DNA found inside most body cells.

CHYME A soup-like liquid that is formed of part-digested food in the stomach and released into the small intestine.

DIAPHRAGM The dome-shaped muscle between the thorax and the abdomen.

DIGESTION The breakdown of the complex molecules in food into simple nutrients, such as sugars, which are absorbed into the bloodstream and used by cells.

DISSECTION The careful cutting open of a dead body to study its internal structure.

DNA (DEOXYRIBONUCLEIC ACID) A molecule containing genes (instructions) for building and running the body's cells.

EMBRYO An unborn baby during the first eight weeks of development after fertilization.

ENDOCRINE GLAND A collection of cells, such as the thyroid gland, that release hormones into the bloodstream.

ENZYME A protein that acts as a biological catalyst to speed up the rate of chemical reactions inside and outside cells.

Model of an enzyme involved in digesting food

FAECES The semi-solid waste made up of undigested food, dead cells, and bacteria, removed from the body through the anus.

FERTILIZATION The fusion of a sperm and an egg to make a new human being.

FETUS A baby growing inside the uterus from its ninth week until its birth.

FOLLICLE A group of cells inside an ova that surrounds and nurtures an egg. Also pit in the skin from which a hair grows.

GAS EXCHANGE The movement of oxyg from the lungs into the bloodstream, and of carbon dioxide from the bloodstream into the lungs.

GENE One of 20,000–25,000 instructions contained within a cell's chromosomes t control its construction and operation.

GLAND A group of cells that create chemical substances, such as hormones or sweat, and release them into the body

GLUCOSE A type of sugar that circulate in the blood and provides cells with their major source of energy.

HOMEOSTASIS The maintenance of sta conditions, such as temperature or amo of water or glucose, inside the body so t cells can work normally.

HORMONE A chemical messenger that made by an endocrine gland and carried the blood to its target tissue or organ.

IMMUNE SYSTEM A collection of cells i the circulatory and lymphatic systems t track and destroy pathogens (germs).

KERATIN The tough, waterproof protei cells that make up the hair, nails, and upper epidermis of the skin.

LYMPH The fluid that flows through the lymphatic system from tissues to the blood.

MEMBRANE A thi layer of tissue tha covers or lines a external or inter body surface. Als cell's outer layer.

MENINGES The protecti membranes that cover the br and spinal cord.

MENSTRUAL CYCLE The sequence body changes, repeated roughly every 2 days, that prepare a woman's reproduct system to receive a fertilized egg.

METABOLISM The chemical processes that take place in every cell in the body, resulting, for example, in the release of energy and growth.

MOLECULE A tiny particle that is made of two or more linked atoms.

NEURON One of the billions of nerve c that make up the nervous system.

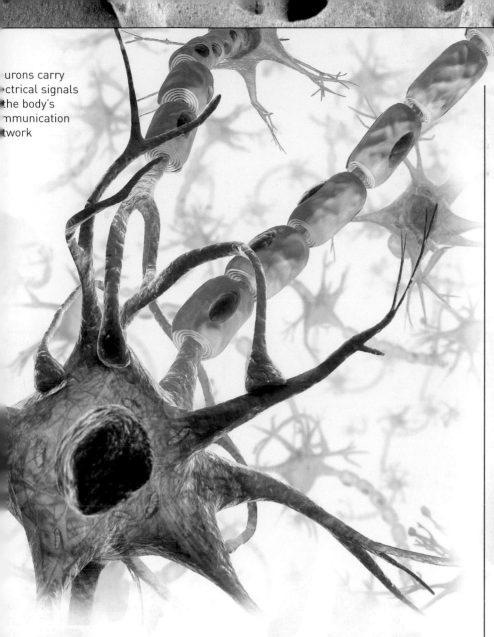

urons carry
ctrical signals
the body's
mmunication
twork

SURGERY The treatment of disease or injury by direct intervention, often using surgical instruments to open the body.

SUTURE An immovable joint such as that between two skull bones.

SYNAPSE A junction between two neurons, where a nerve signal is passed from cell to cell. The neurons are very close at a synapse, but they do not touch.

SYSTEM A collection of linked organs that work together to carry out a specific task or tasks. An example is the digestive system.

TISSUE An organized group of one type of cell, or similar types of cells, that works together to perform a particular function.

TORSO The central part of the body, also known as the trunk, made up of the thorax and abdomen.

UMBILICAL CORD The rope-like structure that connects a fetus to the placenta.

URINE A liquid produced by the kidneys that contains wastes, surplus water, and salts removed from the blood.

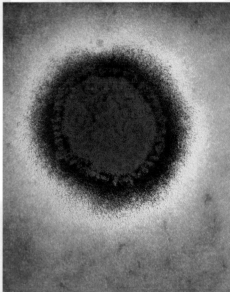

TEM of an influenza (flu) virus magnified 135,000 times

VEIN A blood vessel that carries blood from the body tissues towards the heart.

VIRUS A non-living pathogen that causes diseases, such as colds and measles, in humans.

X-RAY A form of radiation that reveals bones when projected through the body onto film.

TRIENT A substance, such as cose (sugar), needed in the diet aintain normal body functioning good health.

ACTORY To do with the sense mell.

GAN A body part, such as the heart, is made up of two or more types ssue and carries out a icular function.

IFICATION The nation of bone, replacing ilage with bone tissue.

HOGEN A germ, a type icroorganism, such as cterium or virus, that es disease in humans.

SICIAN A doctor.

SIOLOGY The study of ody's functions and esses – how it works.

Sutures, or jigsaw-like joints in the skull

PLACENTA The organ that delivers food and oxygen to a fetus from its mother. Half develops from the mother's body, and half is part of the fetus's body.

PREGNANCY The period of time between an embryo implanting in the uterus and a baby being born, usually 38–40 weeks.

PUBERTY The part of adolescence when a child's body changes into an adult's and the reproductive system starts to work.

SPERM Male sex cells, also called spermatozoa.

SPINAL CORD A column of nervous tissue inside the spine. It relays nerve signals between the brain and body.

Index

A

acupuncture 9, 70
adolescence 63, 70
adrenal glands 40
ageing 63
alveoli 50, 51, 70
amniotic fluid 61, 70
anatomy 6, 10–11, 70
antibodies 45, 70
Aristotle 56
arms 16, 17, 24, 65
arteries 18, 42, 43, 44, 45, 70
atoms 13, 70
Avicenna 8, 9, 66

B

babies 59, 60–61, 62, 64
backbone 16
bacteria 12, 45, 55, 70
Baglivi, Giorgio 22
balance 25, 37
Banting, Sir Frederick 41
Beethoven, Ludwig van 36
Bernard, Claude 55, 67
Best, Charles 41
bile 54, 55, 70
bionic limbs 65
birth 60, 61
bladder 56, 57, 58, 59, 65
blood 9, 46–47, 66
blood clots 47
blood groups 47
blood transfusions 46, 47
blood vessels 6, 19, 29, 33, 44–45, 70
bone marrow 18, 19
bones 6, 16–21, 24, 37
Bowman, William 56, 67
Braille 32
brain 25, 26, 28–31, 65, 66, 67
brain stem 26, 27, 28, 30, 31
breathing 48–51
Broca, Paul Pierre 29, 67

C

capillaries 44, 45, 66, 70
carbon dioxide 48, 50
cartilage 16, 18, 20, 21, 70
cells 7, 12–13, 19, 62, 64, 70
central nervous system 26
cerebellum 26, 27, 28, 30
cerebral cortex 29, 31
cerebrum 26, 27, 28–31
Cesalpino, Andrea 42
Charcot, Jean-Martin 27
Chauliac, Guy de 16
chromosomes 7, 62, 70
chyme 54, 70
circulatory system 44–45
collagen 19, 21
computed tomography (CT) 14, 67
coronary circulation 42
Crick, Francis 62, 67
cyborgs 65

D

diabetes 41
diaphragm 27, 49, 70
digestion 7, 52–55, 70
diseases 8, 45, 64
dissection 6, 10–11, 66, 70
DNA 7, 58, 60, 62, 64, 67, 70
dreams 31

E

ears 36–37
eating 52–53
eggs 58, 59, 60
electron microscopes 13
embalming 8
embryo 18, 60, 64, 70
emotions 31
endocrine system 40–41, 70
endoscopy 15
enzymes 41, 52, 54, 55, 70
epiglottis 48, 49, 53
Eustachio, Bartolomeo 36, 66
eyes 34–35

F

Fabricius, Hieronymus 60, 66
facial muscles 25
faeces 54, 55, 70
feet 16, 21
fertilization 59, 60, 70
fetus 15, 60–61, 63, 70
fingerprints 32, 33
follicles 32, 33, 70
food 52–55
Freud, Sigmund 30

G

Galen, Claudius 8, 9, 10, 66
gall bladder 54, 55
gas exchange 51, 70
genes 7, 62, 64, 70
glands 40–41, 70
glial cells 30
glucose 40, 41, 54, 56, 70
Graaf, Regnier de 59, 66
growth 62–63

H

haemoglobin 47
hair 32, 33
Haller, Albrecht von 44
hands 17, 20, 24, 32, 33
Harvey, William 44, 66
hearing 36–37
heart 6, 42–43, 44, 49, 51
Helmholtz, Hermann von 35, 67
Henle, Jakob 56
hip joint 18, 20
Hippocrates 8, 9, 66
homeostasis 55, 70
Hooke, Robert 12, 66
hormones 40–41, 70
hybrid embryos 64
hypothalamus 30, 40, 41

I J

immune system 45, 46, 70
infections 45
Ingrassias, Giovanni 19
inheritance 62
insulin 41
intelligence 6, 30
intestines 7, 54–55
joints 20–21

K L

keratin 32, 33, 70
kidneys 40, 56–57
knee 20, 21
Landsteiner, Karl 47, 67
larynx 21, 48, 49
Lavoisier, Antoine 50, 66
Leeuwenhoek, Antoni van 12, 66
lifespan 63, 65
ligaments 20, 21, 24
limbic system 30, 31
Liuzzi, Mondino dei 10, 66
liver 52, 54, 56, 67
lungs 6, 42, 43, 48–51
lymph 45, 70
lymphatic system 44, 45
lymphocytes 41, 45, 46, 47

M

macrophages 45
magnetic resonance imaging (MRI) 15, 67
Malpighi, Marcello 12, 66
medicine 8, 9, 64–65
melanin 33, 35
membranes 13, 63, 70
menstrual cycle 59, 70
metabolism 13, 40, 70
microscopes 12–13, 66, 67
milk 61
molecules 7, 70
mouth 52–53
mummies 8–9, 42
muscles 6, 22–25

N

nails 9, 32, 33
nanobots 65
nerves 6, 22, 25, 26–27, 35, 37, 38, 39
nervous system 26–27, 28
neurons 22, 26, 27, 28, 30, 38, 65, 70, 71
nose 38, 48
nutrients 52, 53, 54, 55, 61, 71

O

ophthalmoscopes 14, 35
organs 7, 40, 71
ossification 63, 71
ovaries 40, 58, 59
oxygen 6, 42, 43, 46, 47, 48–49, 50–51

P Q

pancreas 40, 41, 55
pathogens 45, 71
Pavlov, Ivan 26
penis 58
physicians 9, 10–11, 71
physiology 6, 71
pituitary gland 30, 40–41, 59
placenta 61, 71
plasma 46, 47
platelets 46, 47
positron emission tomography (PET) 15, 67
pregnancy 15, 60–61, 70
puberty 63, 71
pulse 42
pupil 35

R

red blood cells 19, 46–47, 51
reflexes 26, 27
Renaissance 6, 10
reproduction 58–61
respiratory system 48–51
retina 34, 35
Roentgen, Wilhelm 14, 67

S

saliva 39, 52, 53
scanning electron micrograph (SEM) 13
senses 32–39
sex cells 58
sight, sense of 34–35
skeleton 6, 16–21, 63
skin 32–33
skull 8, 17, 38, 39, 63
sleep 31
smell, sense of 31, 38
Spallanzani, Lazzaro 50
sperm 12, 58, 59, 60, 71
spinal cord 16, 26, 27, 39, 71
spine 16, 17
stem cells 19, 64
Steno, Nicholas 22
stomach 54
surgery 11, 68, 71
sutures 63, 71
Swammerdam, Jan 25
sweat glands 32
synapses 27, 71
synovial joints 21
systems 7, 71

T

taste, sense of 38–39, 52
tears 34
teeth 52, 53
transmission electron micrograph (TEM) 13, 71
temperature 6, 32, 46
tendons 23, 24
testes 40, 58
thalamus 30
thinking 31
thymus gland 40, 41, 45
thyroid gland 40
tissues 7, 71
tongue 38, 39, 48, 52, 53
torso 62, 71
touch, sense of 32, 33
trachea 21, 48, 49, 50, 51, 67
transplants 65

U V

ultrasound scans 15, 61
umbilical cord 61, 71
urinary system 56–57
urine 56, 57, 71
uterus 58, 59, 60–61
vagina 59
valves, heart 42
veins 19, 42, 43, 44, 45, 66, 71
vertebrae 16, 17
Vesalius, Andreas 10, 58, 66
video pills 15
villi 7, 55
viruses 45, 71
vocal cords 48, 49

W X Y Z

waste disposal 54, 55, 56–57
Watson, James 62, 67
white blood cells 19, 41, 45, 46, 47
X-rays 14, 18, 67, 71

Acknowledgements

Dorling Kindersley would like to thank:
Rajeev Doshi at Medimation (pp.26–27, 28–29, 40–41, and 50–51) & Arran Lewis (pp.38–39) for illustrations; Hilary Bird for the index; David Ekholm- JAlbum, Sunita Gahir, Andrea Mills, Susan St Louis, Lisa Stock, & Bulent Yusuf for the clipart; Sue Nicholson & Edward Kinsey for the wallchart; Monica Byles for proofreading.

For this relaunch edition, the publisher would also like to thank: Camilla Hallinan for text editing, and Carron Brown for proofreading.

The publisher would like to thank the following for their kind permission to reproduce their photographs:

(Key: a-above; b-below/bottom; c-centre; f-far; l-left; r-right; t-top)

akg-images: 9cl, 11tl; **Alamy Images:** Mary Evans Picture Library 9tl, 9tr, 10cl, 12c, 12tl, 18cla, 30cra, 33tr, 34bc, 36tl, 47cl, 56tr; Dennis Hallinan 66bc; INTERPHOTO Pressebildagentur 42br; The London Art Archive 55tr; PHOTOTAKE Inc. 7c, 26bl, 29cra, 60c; The Print Collector 12cb, 16tl, 44cr, 50tr, 56crb, 60cr; Michael Ventura 15tr; World History Archive 29tl; **The Art Archive:** Bodleian Library, Oxford / Ashmole 399 folio 34r, 10tl; Private Collection / Marc Charmet 14tr; **The Bridgeman Art Library:** Bibliothèque de la Faculté de Médecine, Paris / Archives Charmet 46cl; Bibliothèque Nationale, Paris 8cr; Private Collection / Photo Christie's Images 63br; **Corbis:** Bettmann 24tl, 26cl, 41c, 50cl, 67bc; Christophe Boisvieux 31crb; CDC/ PHIL 13tr; EPA / Geoff Caddick 69bl; Frank Lane Picture Agency / Ron Boardman 13crb; The Gallery Collection 31tl, 44clb; Hulton-Deutsch Collection 22tr, 27ca, 49bl; John Zich/zrImages 67br; Gianni Dagli Orti 32c; Reuters / David Gray 69c; Ariel Skelley 62tr; Visuals Unlimited 7cr, 18clb, 19tr; Zefa / Flynn Larsen 33br; **DK Images:** The British Museum, London 42tl; The British Museum, London / Peter Hayman 8–9b, 66cl; Combustion 46–47c, 71tl; Courtesy of Denoyer – Geppert Intl / Geoff Brightling 55bc; Donks Models / Geoff Dann 13c; Arran Lewis 38–39; Linden Artists 57br; Medi-Mation 40–41c, 50–51bc; Courtesy of the Museum of Natural History of the University of Florence, Zoology section 'La Specola' / Liberto Perugi 11cr, 37tc, 44tr; Old Operating Theatre Museum, London / Steve Gorton 2cb, 4tr, 10–11b, 11cl; Courtesy of The Science Museum, London/ Adrian Whicher 8cl; Courtesy of The Science Museum, London / Dave King 3tl, 12cl, 12cr, 66cr, 69cr; Courtesy of The Science Museum, London / John Lepine 67tl; Jules Selmes and Debi Treloar 35tc; **Getty Images:** AFP / Andre Durand 15br; AFP / Damien Meyer 21br; Henry Guttmann 11tr; Hulton Archive 35br; The Image Bank / Johannes Kroemer 70bl; Nick Laham 53tr; Win McNamee 65tl; Michael Ochs Archives 48cb; Popperfoto 28clb; Science Faction / David Scharf 33cr; Science Faction / Rawlins – CMSP 64crb; Stone / Ron Boardman 13bc; Taxi / Emmanuel Faure 15bl; Time Life Pictures / Mansell 37br; Topical Press Agency 41cr; Visuals Unlimited / Michael Gabridge 71bl; **Gunther von Hagens' BODY WORLDS, Institute for Plastination, Heidelberg, Germany, www.bodyworlds.com:** 68b; Courtesy of The Health Museum, Houston: 69tl; **iStockphoto.com:** 8tl; Roberto A. Sanchez 16bl; Jaroslaw Wojcik 64bc; **The Kobal Collection:** Carolco 65bl; Gaumont 46tl; Warner Bros 63tr; **Library Of Congress, Washington, D.C.:** Cornish & Baker 63cr; **Mary Evans Picture Library:** Courtesy of The Old Operating Theatre, Museum & Herb Garret, London: 68tr; **PA Photos:** AP Photo / Brian Walker 65tr; **Photolibrary:** Imagestate / David South 65bc; **Photo Scala, Florence:** The Museum of Modern Art, New York 31cra; **Science Photo Library:** 14cl, 23c, 25tr, 36cla, 59tl; Juergen Berger 64tr; Biology Media 25ca; Dr Goran Bredberg 37cr; A. Barrington Brown 62cla; Scott Camazine, Sue Trainor 18bl; Chemical Design 47cr; CNRI 38bl, 41bc, 49cl, 49fcl; Christian Darkin 65crb; Equinox Graphics 70cb; Eye of Science 55tl; Simon Fraser 15c; GCa 17br; Steve Gschmeissner 19br, 32tr, 51tl; Innerspace Imaging 50bl; ISM / Alain Pol 57cr; Christian Jegou Publiphoto Diffusion 6tl; Nancy Kedersha 30br; James King-Holmes 67cr; Patrick Landmann 64cl; Dr Najeeb Layyous 61tr; Astrid & Hanns-Frieder Michler 41cl; Prof. P. Motta / Dept. of Anatomy / University 'La Sapienza', Rome 39br, 54cl; MPI Biochemistry/ Volker Steger 65c; Dr Gopal Murti 62clb; NIBSC 71cr; Susumu Nishinaga 64–65 (Background), 66–67 (Background), 68–69 (Background), 70–71 (Background); Omikron 35cb; US National Library of Medicine 28tr; Wellcome Department of Cognitive Neurology 15cl; Zephyr 14bc; **Still Pictures:** The Medical File / Charles Brooks 15tl; Ed Reschke 21cb; **Wellcome Library, London:** 6bl, 16cla, 22tl, 23b, 23tc, 36cb, 38tc, 42tr.

© 2008, by SOMSO models, www.somso.com: 2tr, 3tr, 4cla, 4cra, 18cr, 19ca, 24c, 27br, 30bl, 31bc, 32bl, 46bl, 53bc, 53bl, 56bl, 56br, 58br, 59br, 60b, 61bl.

Wallchart: DK Images: Denoyer - Geppert Intl. br (inner ear). **Science Photo Library:** ftr (cell division).

All other images
© Dorling Kindersley
For further information see:
www.dkimages.com